In loving memories of Gene Jaeger
Florence E. Jaeger

$24⁰⁰

AF081855

FLAT-BOTTOM ODYSSEY

Aboard LST 400
From North Africa to D-Day

A MEMOIR

By Gene Jaeger

Lieut., USNR
Executive Officer, USS LST 400

"It seems the fate of two empires rests on some damned thing called an LST."
— *Winston Churchill, 1942*

Prairie Ocean Press
Henry, Illinois

© 2010 by Gene Jaeger

Prairie Ocean Press
1101 School Street
Henry, Illinois 61537
g.jaeger@mchsi.com

ISBN: 978-0-692-00895-9

All maps are by Betsy Jaeger Lawson.

Photo acquisition and research, by Betsy Jaeger Lawson, made use of the following sources:

Naval History and Heritage Command, Online Library of Selected Images, Photographic Section at http://www.history.navy.mil

National Archives Still Picture Branch at http://www.archives.gov/research/ww2/photos

NavSource Naval History - Photographic History of the U.S. Navy at http://www.navsource.org

Wikimedia Commons, an online repository of free-use images for Wikipedia articles or for off-site use, under GNU free documentation license, Creative Commons attribution/share-alike licenses or public domain. For more information, see Wikimedia Commons under Wikipedia at http://www.wikipedia.org

Geneva in Vintage Postcards, by John J. Laukaitis, Arcadia Publishing, Charleston, SC, 2004, ISBN 0-7385-3347-5

Our Prairie Shipyard, Historical Edition, Vol. IV, June 1945, No. 5 Chicago Bridge and Iron Company—Seneca Shipyard (CB&I)

Production Services: Populore® Publishing Company, Morgantown, West Virginia

Dedication

In dedicating this book to the young soldiers, sailors and airmen who met the enemy face to face in World War II, it is tempting to use the ornate language of the professional patriot, but those guys didn't talk that way. In fact, I never heard one of them put his feelings about the war into words. But they knew. When your home, family and friends are threatened you don't talk; you fight. John Steinbeck described them best:

> *"They fought the war of homesick, weary, funny, violent, common men…who lug themselves through as dirty a business as the world has ever seen and do it with humor and dignity and courage."*

Contents

Preface vii

Acknowledgments ix

Introduction 1

A New Kind of War 7

Atlantic Ocean 25

Sicily 37

After the Battle 53

Italy 69

United Kingdom 81

Prelude to Normandy 97

D-Day and Beyond 107

Stateside 129

Anti-Climax 139

Preface

The December 7, 1941 attack on Pearl Harbor confronted the United States with a unique problem. The Axis Powers had seized lands, nations and islands that must be freed. The U.S. had done a similar job in 1917–1918 with one significant difference. The Doughboys and their weapons were welcomed at European seaports; the G.I.s were not. At the end of 1941, the European and Pacific ports were held by the enemy.

The heavy weapons needed to re-take the captured lands would have to be delivered in flat-bottomed, bow-loading ships that could load 20 Sherman tanks in Philadelphia and deliver them, under fire, on hostile beaches. The ships needed then are now called LSTs (Landing Ship, Tanks), but on December 7, 1941, the only LST that existed was still on a drawing board. The Pearl Harbor attack sparked a spectacular burst of productivity. The design work was completed, bottoms were laid in several shipyards throughout the U.S. and the first LSTs were launched in December 1942.

With these unique, 328-foot, flat-bottom ships coming on line, the Navy needed 100,000 men to run them. Training for this job would call for experienced instructors and plenty of time. The Navy had neither. But the war couldn't wait. If trained men weren't available to run the LSTs, untrained men would have to do it. This is the story of those untrained men going into battle in untried ships; the men called upon to do on-the-job training and fight a war in the process.

Our ship, the LST 400, was commissioned in Newport News on January 7, 1943. It went into battle in Sicily six months later. Its story moves from our learning the difference between port and starboard to our first storm at sea and then to firing at enemy bombers and sweating U-Boat attacks. The raw, young crew that commissioned LST 400 was soon involved in the battle of North Africa followed by D-Day landings at Sicily, Italy and Normandy. The war in Europe won, these seasoned, but still youthful, veterans were immediately called upon to form the nucleus of new crews needed to storm Japanese beaches. This is a story of the horror and absurdity of war. It's also a story of the youth who endured it with spirit and even, God knows how, with humor.

Gene Jaeger
October 2009

Acknowledgments

With gratitude:

To my first reader, prime supporter and wife, Florence Jaeger.

To Betsy Jaeger Lawson, who not only helped the book take shape but also encouraged and enlightened the author every step of the way.

To Bob Wilson, the Sage of Saxtons River, Vermont, for the guidance drawn from his years of devotion to the written word.

Lieutenant Gene Jaeger, USNR, Executive Officer, 1945, USS LST 400 (courtesy of the author)

Introduction

Recently I stood on the upland prairie overlooking the Illinois River just above Peoria. I was watching an unusual ship work its way upstream. Most Illinois River traffic is made up of double-ended barges loaded with grain, oil and chemicals, and pushed by towboats. But this was no towboat. It was a seagoing ship with a high, rounded bow and an after deckhouse. I had seen this ship before. The year was 1943. The ship was the LST 325. It had just been commissioned by the U.S. Navy and was doing its shakedown cruise on lower Chesapeake Bay.

What is (or was) an LST? Probably I should stay in the past tense because the ship I was looking at is the only one left of a fleet of more than a thousand that sailed the globe in the cataclysmic 1940s. The LST was a cargo ship but unlike any cargo ships I had ever seen. A typical cargo ship has a keel, draws 25 feet of water and loads through hatches in its main deck. An LST had a flat bottom, sailed in only nine feet of water and loaded through huge doors in its bow. It also had a battery of anti-aircraft guns. This ungainly but versatile vessel could carry anything to anyplace, but what it did best was carry arms and men to beaches where they weren't welcome.

The need for LSTs was perceived by Winston Churchill in 1941. He was reported to have said, in scriptural tones: "Let there be built great ships which can cast upon a beach large numbers of the heaviest tanks." Probably apocryphal, but Sir Winston did lean toward the superlative. At his urging, the British modified three shallow-draft tankers for beaching. They were said to have worked fairly well, but they made it clear that the design of a truly effective landing ship would have to

November, 1941 (from Wikimedia Commons 3.0)

June, 1942 (courtesy of CB&I)

December, 1942 (courtesy of CB&I)

June, 1943 (courtesy of CB&I)

start with the hull. Short of materials and shipyard space, the British turned to the United States. In November, 1941 the U.S. Navy Bureau of Ships assigned the LST design job to John Neidermair. In a few weeks Neidermair produced drawings of a 328-foot, flat-bottomed ship with an enclosed tank deck that could carry 20 Sherman tanks to a beach and discharge them through open bow doors. This highly functional ugly duckling was called a Landing Ship, Tanks (LST).

The first LST bottom was laid down in Newport News, Virginia on June 10, 1942. The USS LST 1 was commissioned at the Dravo Shipyard in Pittsburgh on the following December 14th. LSTs made their first attack against Axis forces at Sicily on July 10, 1943, thirteen months after the first bottom was laid.

In all, 1051 LSTs were built. Almost all of them saw action; about sixty were lost. The single LST afloat and able to move under its own power is LST 325, now moored on the Ohio River at Evansville, Indiana. The 325 cruises the inland waterways where it commands public attention as a war memorial. It commands my attention as a comrade-in-arms. I first saw it in January, 1943, from the bridge of a sister-ship, LST 400. Both ships had been recently commissioned and their young crews were learning to run them. Later the 325 and the 400 traveled in the same convoys, fired at the same bombers and enjoyed the same liberty ports until the final days of the war in Europe.

What follows is my recollection of WWII in Europe as seen from the bridge of the LST 400. In telling this story I don't try to explain amphibious warfare or give the details of a particular beachhead assault. I have no more knowledge of those things now than I did in 1944. I recall a visit to my father's office in Chicago after the war. His colleagues pressed me for details of the Normandy invasion and I soon became aware that they knew more about the invasion than I did. The American public closely followed newspapers and radio accounts of the war. Many had maps hung on their living room walls. They knew about the St. Lo breakthrough and about Monty's difficulties at Caen. I could tell them only about the piece of water we floated on and about what I saw on the shoreline in front of me and the threatening sky above me. I told them what I knew of the ugly things lurking in the sea below. Those limitations still apply. I write here about the ship, its crew and myself: where we went, what we did and what we saw. I mention other ships only to the extent that they thrust themselves into my story. I mention the Pacific war hardly at all. I wasn't there.

This is a story about what one civilian-turned-sailor saw in a few isolated spots in the midst of worldwide calamity—the greatest catastrophe mankind has ever known.

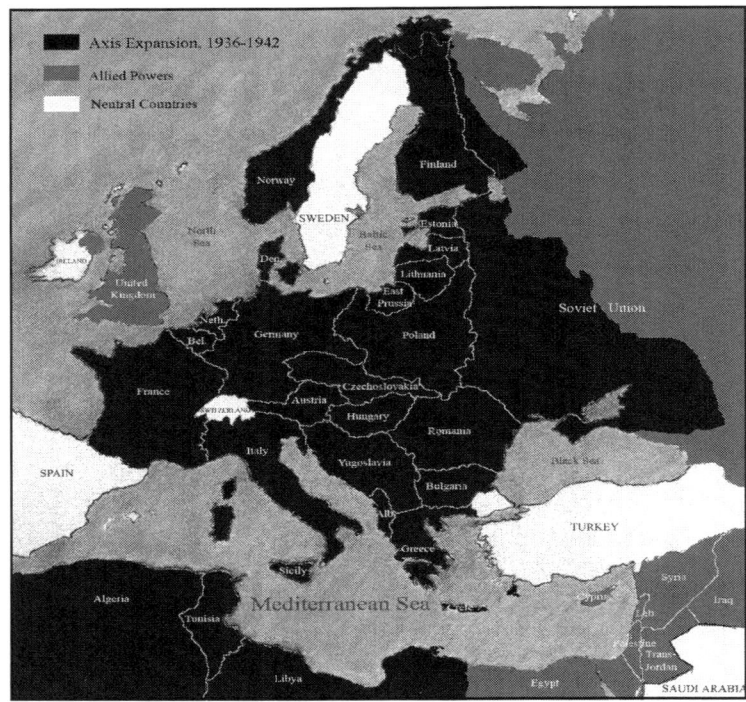

Axis Expansion, 1936–1942

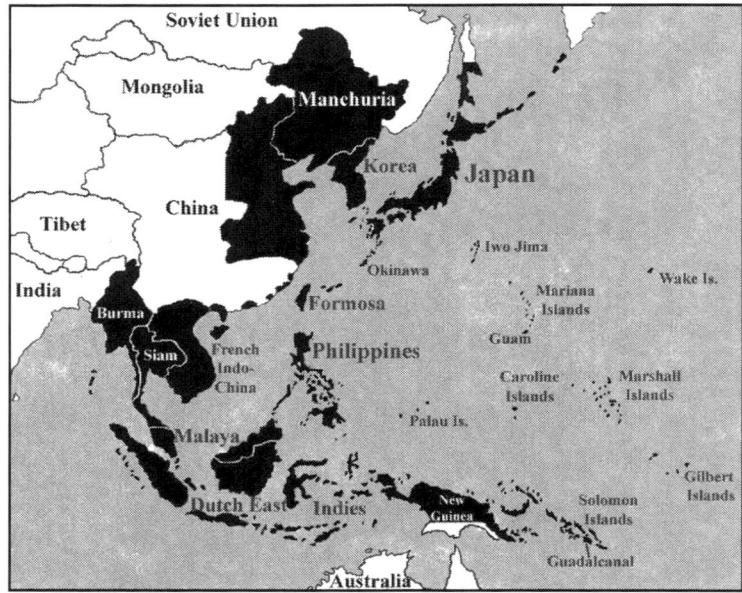

The Japanese Empire, 1942

CHAPTER 1

A New Kind of War

World War II began with Axis powers seizing western Europe and large areas of the western Pacific Ocean. The summer of 1942 marked a turning point. The Germans still occupied Europe and the north coast of Africa, but their drive into the Soviet Union was blunted by the Russian stand at Stalingrad in August. Japanese expansion in the Pacific was halted by the U.S. Navy's defeat of a Japanese aircraft carrier task force at Midway on June 4 and the U.S. landing on Guadalcanal in August.

My own Navy career began at the Board of Trade Building in Chicago in June of 1942. I had just graduated from Notre Dame where I had taken flying lessons, courtesy of a foresighted government. I'm sure I was expected to join an air force if war broke out and that's exactly what I was doing in Chicago that day, or trying to. The Navy was the air force of my choice for no other reason than that's where many of my classmates were going. My fate was decided on the 22nd floor. There I was given an eye test that required me to line up two eight-inch sticks, about ten feet distant, by drawing on attached strings.

"No go," said the medic. "Next."

Out in the hall a few minutes later, a name caught my eye: Lieutenant Commander Jones. The night before, my uncle had told me: "When you're in the Board of Trade tomorrow, look up Jones." Apparently they'd had a drink together earlier in the week. It couldn't hurt so I knocked on the door. The Commander was cordial. Regards to the uncle and what can I do for

Geneva in 1869 (courtesy of John J. Laukaitis, Ph.D.)

you. I told him that the Navy Air Force had decided to get along without me and I was looking for something to do. He told me to look in on Lieutenant Smith in Room 2212. Smith was looking for officers to do courier duty. That sounded good. I saw myself being flown to London to deliver top-secret messages to General Eisenhower. The Lieutenant was out but his yeoman gave me application papers and I took the next train home.

Home was Geneva, Illinois, a village on the wooded slopes of the Fox River, 36 miles west of Chicago. It was a typical river valley town, starting in 1832 with a cabin on the west side of a shallow river crossing. Soon there were a dozen cabins, a general store and a mill dam. Similar towns grew up along the river and the surrounding prairie was plowed into cropland.

I came on the scene in 1920 in Ottawa, Illinois, moving north in the late 20s. Geneva was then a town of 4,200 with an unusual ethnic mix: the founding WASPs, the Scandinavian arrivals of the 1880s and the Italian latecomers at the turn of the century. In the 1930s Swedish accents could be heard at city council meetings, and the parents of my Italian schoolmates still spoke their native tongue. The Swedish-Italian mix was a healthy one. My contemporaries included handsome children bearing names like Mario Swanson and Ingrid Nottolini. It was a tolerant community. During my years there, Geneva voters elected Catholic, Protestant and Jewish mayors.

I passed from boyhood to manhood in the "turbulent thirties." That's an expression I read in a book. Those years certainly weren't turbulent for me. If I had given newspapers more than a passing glance when I was a boy I would have known that people were actually starving in the cities. No such troubles were apparent in Geneva. Besides, depressions were things for adults to worry about. Three meals a day, clean clothes, a warm bed—those things just weren't my problem. I did become vaguely aware that there were needy people in town when I saw a classmate wearing a sweater my cousin had discarded the previous year. Apparently the adults knew what was going on. It was years before I became aware that my father had almost lost his politically appointed job in the 1932 change of administrations.

Even mandatory schooling didn't disturb my serenity. Classes were dreamy affairs and I don't recall that home study was required. At least I never did any. What I did do was wander about the woods and creeks and, my prime love, the river. When I wasn't doing that I was at the library where I read, on the average, three adventure stories a week. College added beer drinking to my pastimes and *Beowulf* and *The Odyssey* to my adventure stories. It didn't much change my outlook. Hitler's invasion of Poland didn't ruffle my detachment even though my classmates were beginning to talk about their future in the military. Europe was a long way off. I wrote what I considered to be a humorous piece comparing RAF victories in the Battle of Britain to the batting averages of our major league baseball players. "Not funny," said the good father correcting my essay, using his red pencil for a one-paragraph lecture on human compassion. I believe he used the word "callous."

After my call on the Navy in Chicago, I didn't give my military situation much thought. I knew the draft board would resolve the matter in good time. I needed some spending money so I took a night job at a foundry. Dirty work, but I had been there before. The big drawback to the foundry job was the night hours. I got off at midnight and by the time I showered and got downtown my only companions were the town drunks. I also worked briefly for a concrete contractor building a new war plant. Jobs were plentiful now; the depression was over. One day I was pouring concrete for the floor of the boiler room when I saw my friend Keith Murray climbing down the ladder to join me. We were in the same boat—waiting for the call up. That was the last I saw of Keith. He was killed on a beach in Italy the following year.

In late August I received a large, brown paper envelope with the paperwork commissioning me an ensign in the U.S. Naval Reserve. No mention of training or of an indoctrination period. *Now*. In fact I had been a Navy officer for the past week while I was busy shoveling sand. A few days later I received written orders to report to Princeton University in ten days—in uniform. I borrowed a hundred bucks from my father, which I turned over to Marshall Fields in Chicago for a set of khakis and a dress blue uniform with a single gold stripe on the sleeve. Dressed for the first time in military garb, I set out for Chicago to catch the New York Central (or was it the Pennsy) to Princeton. I felt guilty whenever an enlisted man saluted, wondering what he would have thought if he knew he had just saluted a foundry hand. The casual commission wasn't unusual in those days. Military assignments were sometimes erratic and it worked both ways. I heard of a guy whose record included prepping at exclusive Baker School in Massachusetts. He wound up in the galley.

The Princeton of F. Scott Fitzgerald's *This Side of Paradise* appealed to me. I saw myself drinking beer at the Nass with the sons of eastern grandees. What I got was a bunk in a small room with three other guys in Patton Hall. From there we were marched to and from classes and the dining hall (not yet the mess hall). Classes were routine. The course in Navy Regulations was called "Rocks and Shoals" because an early line read:

Patton Hall at Princeton University (courtesy of Goody Clancy, Architects)

"…the Commanding Officer shall not suffer his ship to be run onto rocks and shoals" or words to that effect. That, and a few other courses, were designed to give a Navy-officer veneer to the 30-year-old teachers, lawyers and accountants who made up the class. These men were prepping for non-combat jobs in supply, office management, public relations and the like. As a 22-year-old, I was out of place with these family men in mid-career, but my situation was consistent with my aborted experience in the Board of Trade Building in June. Lieutenant Smith had never seen me and whoever read my application papers probably overlooked my birth date. Healthy young specimens like myself were supposed to be sent to the 90 Day Wonder program for training as deck officers. But there I was, on track to an exciting but comfortable career delivering Ike's mail.

And then, that Churchill again. This time, under pressure from Stalin, the PM reportedly said: "Up until last year, I never thought much about LSTs, but now the whole damn war depends on them." A new kind of war. In the past, nations marched their armed forces into battle or used open ports to unload their men and arms. Even in World War I, the Allies debarked their armies at Le Havre, Cherbourg, Brest and other friendly European ports. In 1943 the Allies were denied those ports and required to force their way into Europe over enemy held beaches, using shallow draft ships—LSTs. General George Marshall added his authoritarian voice: "I have studied every aspect of land warfare in my military career, but never amphibious tactics. Now I think of nothing else."

In that climate we should have seen it coming. On graduation day we were given orders sending the whole damned class to Little Creek, Virginia. The Amphibious Force! The moaning of the teachers, lawyers and accountants was piteous. As for me—what the hell—the Navy Air Force could make it on its own; Ike could find another mailman. Fate had me marked for a deck officer all along.

The Princeton tradition didn't elude me entirely. I did get to the Nass one night to hear students sing a song whose refrain still rests gentle on my mind: "That Sonofabitch The Bastard King of England." I also took my first step toward becoming a mariner. I took a train to Manhattan and boarded the Staten Island ferry. Half way across the bay I went to the upper deck, peered over the port bow, down through the Narrows and saw—the Atlantic Ocean. A lubber no longer.

My orders allowed me ten days to report to Little Creek (part of the Norfolk Naval Operating Base) so I headed home. Air travel was restricted to high priority passengers so I had to settle for an 18-hour ride in a crowded coach car on the Pennsylvania Railroad from Philadelphia to Chicago. I was lucky to get a seat; there were actually standees on that train. By the time we reached Indiana the passengers were getting on each others' nerves. A loud mouthed, drunken soldier was particularly obnoxious and a young officer told him to quiet down. The soldier, seeing no MPs, told the officer to go to hell—and got away with it. A lesson there. Your authority is only as strong as your backup.

I saw few friends on the streets of Geneva when I arrived. The U.S. had been at war for almost a year and the young men were in the service. That's where the civilians expected them to be. It was not unusual for the mother of a serviceman to ask a mufti-clad male: "Why aren't you in uniform?" My older brother, Jack, took a lot of heat on that score. He had lost a kidney in an accident and the armed forces wouldn't even consider his efforts to enlist, but what the public saw was a healthy young athlete in civilian clothes. Jack told me of a time when he and his bride accompanied another couple to Chicago to see the young husband off on a train to Fort Bragg. The train pulled out and Jack left the station with an attractive girl on each arm. A soldier with a duffel on his back and orders in his pocket confronted him: "How *do* you do it." Jack had a more serious encounter on a train to St. Paul where he had a job designing sleds for arctic warfare. Drunken GIs blocked his passage through a crowded coach. Verbal abuse threatened to become physical when a sergeant put an end to the squabble.

My family and I knew where I was heading and that I probably wouldn't be back for years, if at all. The farewells were brief and unemotional and I was soon pulling out of Chicago's Union Station on another crowded passenger train, this time headed for Norfolk. This trip was more tedious than the last one. I was happy to get off that train and stretch my legs on the shores of Hampton Roads. I had never heard that name and I made enquiries to learn that this was the James River estuary into Chesapeake Bay, one of the largest harbors in the world. Seaports such as Norfolk, Portsmouth and Newport News ringed this body of water. I was soon to know them all.

I showed my orders to the duty officer at the Navy Base. He directed me to a room with a table, a few chairs and four ensigns (not flags, Navy officers). We did a little verbal sparring with the easy familiarity of strangers who find themselves in the same predicament. We had no reason to believe then that the five of us would spend the next two-and-a-half years living out of one another's mess kits. Our little cadre was just what my Princeton experience would lead me to expect: a lawyer, an accountant, a teacher, an engineer and a foundry hand.

The five of us were startled when a yeoman (a petty officer who does the paper work) stuck his head in the door to tell us that our crew was ready and waiting at a place called Solomons, Maryland. Things moved fast in Norfolk. We were bussed to Little Creek where we boarded an LCI along with 25 other new officers. At sunset, the LCI (Landing Craft, Infantry) had cleared the Little Creek jetty and was headed north on Chesapeake Bay. At midnight we were surprised to see a flashing light on the starboard bow. The skipper, a former Chesapeake boatman, now a Navy officer, told us that the light was a distress signal. We headed for it and soon came upon a trawler with a single crewman. The boat was lying low in the water but not in serious trouble. While the boatman described his plight to the skipper, his eyes kept shifting to the 30 officers, all in dress blue, staring down at him from the darkened ship. All seamen have heard tales of ghost ships with phantom crews. Whatever the fisherman thought, he suddenly decided that he could reach Cape Charles Village on his own and vanished into the night. We reached Solomons next morning without further incident.

Crew #3051 was waiting for their new officers in a gymnasium. LSTs were now coming on the line at the rate of about five a week. The demand for crews to man them was urgent and new sailors were pouring out of boot camps at San Diego, Great Lakes and Newport by the thousands. Well, they looked like sailors. They wore white Navy caps and bell-bottomed trousers but, in fact, none of these 18- to 20-year-olds had ever set foot on the deck of a ship. They were called apprentice seamen after six weeks in boot camp where they learned to say "yes sir" and "no sir" and to mop wooden floors. Later they would say "swab the decks." I'm sure the Navy did its damnedest to put the right man in the right job, but the Bureau of Personnel was overwhelmed. Personnel officers often prepared ship rosters with a scissors. Need 75 men? Just clip that many names off this morning's roll call and hand it to the yeoman. Our ship once

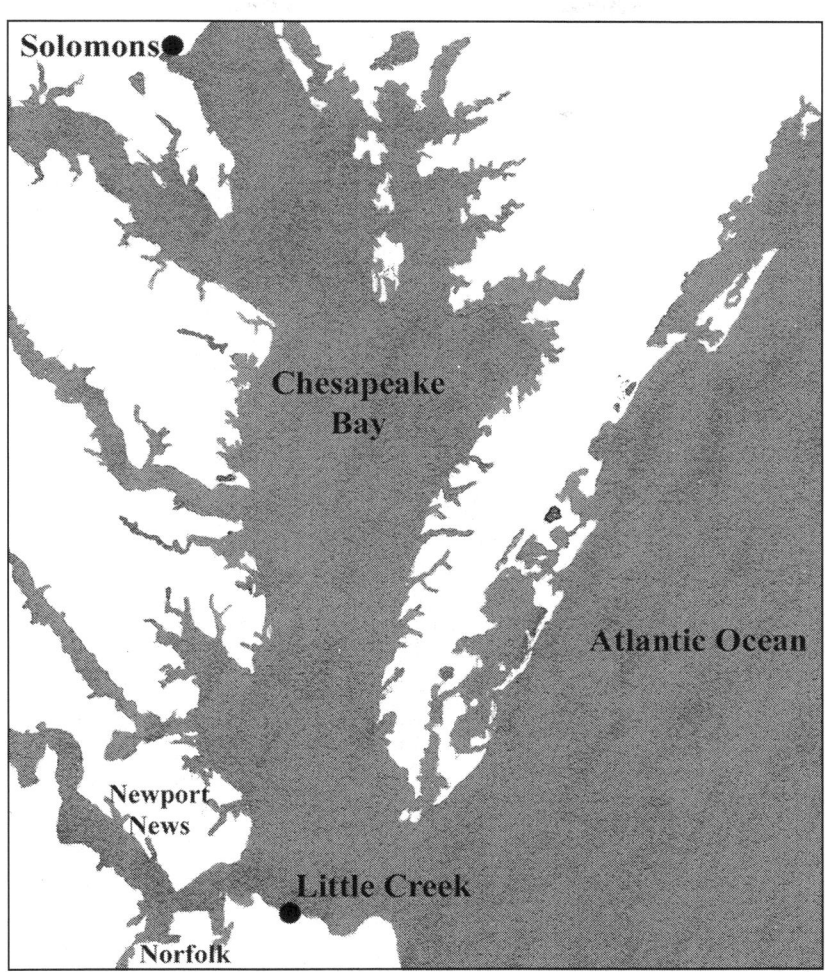

Lower Chesapeake Bay: *In early 1943 the newly created LSTs trained off Little Creek Navy Base on the southern shore of Chesapeake Bay. Their crews were organized at Solomons, Maryland, 100 miles up the bay.*

received 17 replacements from boot camp. Each man's name began with an "M."

We crossed the gym to our waiting crew trying to think of something to say to them. We decided that roll call would be appropriate and authoritative, even if meaningless. I was pondering calisthenics when we were ordered to board an LST about to shove off on a training cruise. That was more like it. We spent the day watching another training group operate the ship under the watchful eyes of an experienced (about three weeks) crew. Eager for more, we returned to the barracks where we were told to pick up our orders from the duty officer. Crew #3051 was ordered back to Norfolk to pick up their new ship.

"This can't be," I told the duty officer, "this crew isn't trained yet."

"If these orders say they're trained, they're trained," he replied. "Your transportation will be here at 0800. Be at the dock."

To make matters worse, the duty officer insisted on a short-arm inspection before the crew left the base. I had to ask a crew member what the hell a short-arm inspection was. Turned out to be a venereal disease check—not part of my curriculum at Notre Dame. The crew groaned. "For chrissake Mr. Jaeger," said one, "We been short-armed three times in the last two days and we haven't been off the base."

On January 7, 1943, we stood at attention aboard the USS LST 400, moored portside to a dock in the Newport News Shipyard. Thank God the Navy had seen fit to furnish us with a chief boatswain (bosun), a chief motor machinist and a shiny new two-stripe captain. The ship itself was fresh as paint. The commissioning ceremony was brief, marred only by the fact that at the first flag raising, the stars and stripes were hoisted upside down—the international distress signal. That was corrected and a letter from the authorities was read, placing the ship in our hands with orders to defend our country against its enemies. Impressive.

With the commissioning ceremony behind us, it was time to set the first watch. The new commanding officer stood on the flag deck with the executive officer, a few seamen and me. He held an organization sheet in one hand and the ship's roster in the other. The organization sheet called for a man to serve as messenger on the bridge. The skipper glanced at the roster, turned to the nearest seaman and barked his first order: "Go get Scalamoni." The kid wheeled and dashed for the ladder where he paused, turned and headed back. "I'm Scalamoni."

Our second skipper came aboard about three weeks after the ship was commissioned. In the Navy, when not addressing the captain directly, it was customary to refer to him as the "old man." Our "old man" was 26 years old. His name was Charles J. Lyden, a geologist and mining engineer in civilian life. He was aboard the USS *California* when it was bombed at Pearl Harbor. Duty as a junior officer on a battleship would hardly qualify him as commanding officer of an LST, but what he lacked in experience he made up for in brains and guts. He led us through

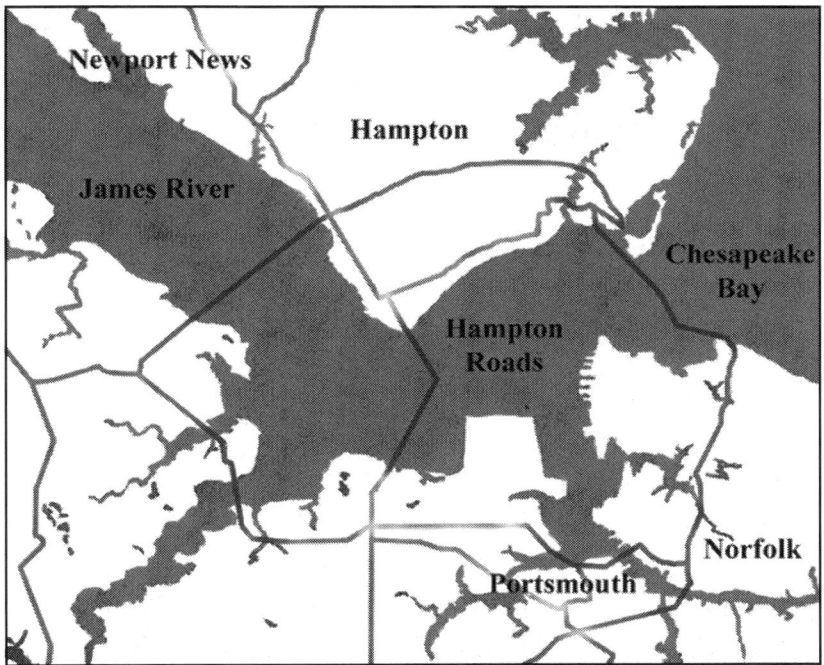

Newport News and Norfolk, Virginia: LST 400 was launched at the Newport News Shipyard, provisioned at the Norfolk Navy Base and did her training in Chesapeake Bay.

the entire war in Europe, landed 50 loads of men and war materials on enemy shores and never lost a man.

We took our new ship out through the submarine nets that opened from Hampton Roads into Chesapeake Bay. It was there that I first saw LST 325. Training was brief. We beached twice on Chesapeake's south shore and fired our 20 mm guns at a sleeve towed by low flying aircraft from the Norfolk Operating Base. We were told that Navy fliers flew those missions as a punishment. We also had a 3", 50 caliber cannon mounted on our stern. We never fired it this side of the Atlantic. Most of our time was spent tied to a pier at Lambert's Point where truck after truck rolled out on the dock to fill our apparently limitless holds. Each officer was responsible for seeing that his division was fully supplied. Each officer had heard the horror story of the ship that had left port without a single roll of toilet paper aboard. We each requisitioned a full ration for our division. The base interpreted each requisition as a full ship's ration. When LST 400 was decommissioned in Taiwan 40 years later, it still had a ten-year supply of toilet paper.

Our loading was interrupted when we were boarded by a harbor pilot who brought the ship to a horseshoe-shaped dock called a deperming station. There, highly charged electrical cables were placed about the ship to reduce its magnetic field. It was necessary to take sensitive instruments out of the range of the cables' powerful energy field. It was my job as Officer-of-the-Deck to note the removal of each instrument in the ship's log. My sea lingo wasn't highly developed yet and I was stopped cold when the quartermaster removed a pair of eight-inch iron spheres from the compass binnacle. I called over to the exec: "Jim, what do you call these things?" He told me. The log, now in naval archives, still reads: *watches, chronometers, magnetic compasses, clocks, navigator's balls and Flanders Bars removed from ship.*

By the end of March, we were moored again at Lambert's Point, our loading completed. The only noteworthy event was a fight on the dock between two sailors from another ship. I was the only officer present and it was clearly my job to break it up. Remembering the incident on the train, I looked carefully around to make sure there were petty officers within calling range, and then stepped in. The warriors quit swinging at each other and turned to verbal warfare. That was out of my jurisdiction so I continued down the dock. The reason that trivial incident sticks in my mind is because the sailors were *going* on liberty, not returning.

The extensive loading and the meager training came to an end on March 23rd when we were again boarded by a pilot. This one took us across Hampton Roads to Portsmouth Navy Yard where we tied up under the hugest crane any of us had ever seen. Its job was to pick up a 120-foot, 900-ton LCT and place it on our main deck. LCT 461 was a smaller, shallower draft version of our own ship. Note the fine distinction in naval terminology. The LCT was a landing *craft*/tanks; the LST was a landing *ship*/tanks. I was told that a craft is a vessel of less than 200 feet in length; a ship of more than 200 feet. LCTs could carry five tanks. They were invaluable in landing arms on beaches out of reach of the deeper draft LSTs. With LCT 461 securely lashed to our deck, we were ready for sea.

Our convoy formed just outside of Cape Charles and Cape Henry. At that time no shipping moved on the North Atlantic without an anti-submarine escort. The escort, or screen, consisted of a ring of about a dozen destroyers, patrol craft and an occasional Canadian corvette (sub-chaser). The screening ships were equipped with sounding gear (sonar), depth charge and 3" caliber guns to keep the wolf packs of U-Boats at bay. Convoy sizes varied. I recall convoys of eight columns with ten ships in a column. Some were much larger. At sea, the ship's crew was divided into three watches. Each watch took four hour turns as the duty watch which operated the engines and manned the wheelhouse, the signal bridge and the radio shack. The off-duty watches did their division chores and managed to do some sleeping and eating.

If you could keep the U-Boats out-of-mind, the trip to New York was a pleasant one. The weather was fair. On the portside

LCT 461 placed on main deck of LST 400 on March 23, 1943

The trio on the main deck, looking over the bow (l–r) are George Doane, Dennis, MA; J. G. Hamblin, Cambridge, VT; unknown.

The couple standing on the bow ramp (l–r) are G. Scalamoni, MA; Robert Brown, Hanson, MA.

Seated on the gangplank rail, just inboard of the guy in the white shirt is Joe Burba, Colchester, CT.

(courtesy of the Mariner's Museum, Newport News, VA)

we could make out buildings on the Atlantic coast. Best of all we were doing a reasonable job of running a Navy ship. The engine room crew (black gang) had the diesels driving; cooks were cooking; signalmen, radiomen and lookouts were on the job; and the officers of the deck were holding position in convoy. The charts showed us to be passing Assateague Island, Delaware Bay and Atlantic City, fascinating names for us inlanders. Then came Rockaway Point and Sandy Hook followed by the Ambrose Lightship whose flashing light (in peacetime) marked the entrance to New York Harbor. The lightship has long since been replaced by electronic satellite devices that can pinpoint a ship's position on the darkest night. I hope Ambrose Lightship is

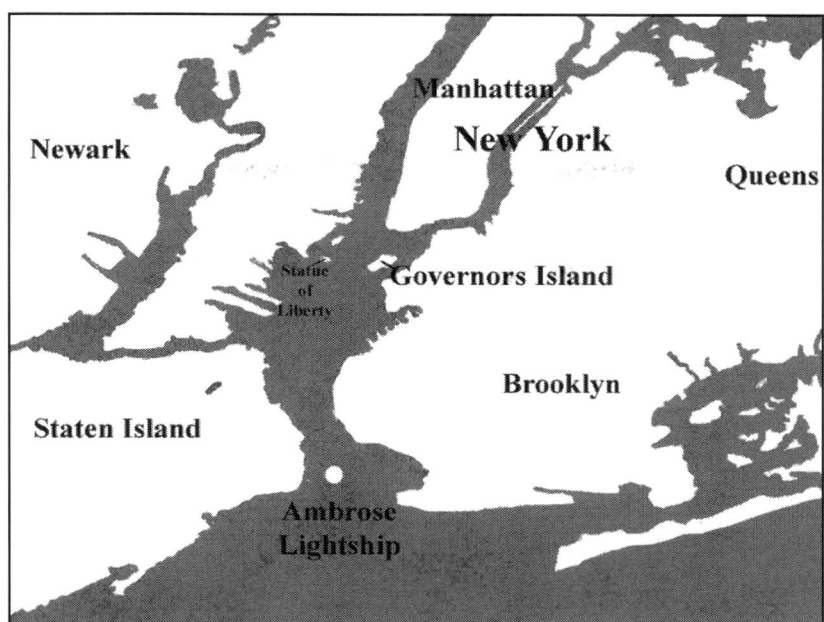

New York Harbor

resting comfortably somewhere. It, like the lighthouses, should be remembered for precious years of service and beauty.

Upper New York Harbor is not for amateurs. The Hudson River flows toward the sea, tidal currents flow from the sea and the flow from the East River crosses them both. Then there's the traffic. Cargo ships, warships and garbage scows moved up and down the rivers while ferries and tugboats crossed it. Ship handling in this confinement required great skill and experience. All seagoing vessels entering or leaving the upper bay required a New York Harbor pilot. Even the captain of the *Queen Mary* turned control over to the pilot. I was told that the pilot's association was close knit. You had to be born into it.

We picked up our pilot somewhere near the lightship. With the pilot at the conn, the bridge crew was relaxed enough to enjoy the sight of the Statue of Liberty off the port bow, the tall Manhattan buildings dead ahead and Governors Island off to starboard. We dropped the hook (Navy talk for anchoring; I was pretty salty by this time) in a stretch of water called Buttermilk

Channel, between Governors Island and South Brooklyn. Ships rode at anchor as far as I could see. A cluster of LSTs lay nearby, apparently part of the oversea convoy we had come to join. At this point, all convoy personnel was confined to ship. I was our ship's communication officer at that time and in that capacity I was sent ashore for our written orders. I picked the orders up somewhere in the Battery and delivered them to the captain. Nothing surprising. We were ordered to sortie (good word) off Sandy Hook in Convoy BRG bound for Gibraltar.

Our next port of call would be in North Africa, but one passenger had different plans. From our starboard bridge wing I could see a patrol boat moving away from our anchorage toward an object in the water near the Brooklyn shore. With binoculars, I could just make out a swimmer. The patrol boat soon had him aboard. I suspect that the swimmer was a sailor or soldier trying to make it ashore to his Brooklyn home. If so, what would you call him? A deserter in time of war? A scared kid trying to escape a situation he didn't understand and couldn't cope with? I remember hoping that the authorities took it easy on him.

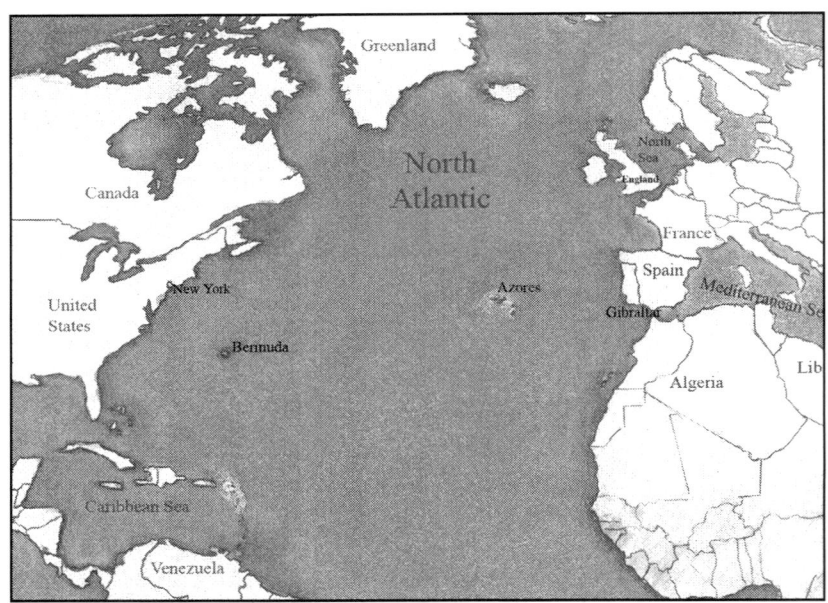

Battle of the Atlantic

CHAPTER 2

Atlantic Ocean

On November 4, 1942, The British 8th Army defeated German forces at El Alamein. Four days later the Americans landed at Casablanca. On May 12, 1943, the German army was driven out of North Africa. The Battle of the North Atlantic (U-Boats) peaked in 1943. In the Pacific, Guadalcanal fell to American Forces.

On or about the first of May our too brief stay in New York came to an end. Freighters, tankers and LSTs moved down through the Narrows into the open sea, feeling their ways to appointed positions in the Gibraltar-bound convoy. The mission had begun. Our job was to carry men and materials to the enemy shore. The enemy's job was to stop us—and they had the weapons to do it. The German surface fleet was held in check in the North Sea by the Royal Navy and we were still out of the Luftwaffe's range, but their *Unterseeboots* were raising hell with our convoys. Our fleets of cargo ships were getting across but often with serious losses. The Allied Merchant Marine lost over 1,000 ships and nearly 10,000 men in World War II.

LST 400's position in the convoy was "4-6," that is, the sixth ship in the fourth column. We had developed the knack of keeping station, an important factor. A tight formation of ships was easier for the screen to protect. The officer-of-the-deck's (OOD) job was to hold the ship in line at a 600-foot interval from the ship ahead. He did this from the conning tower by issuing orders through a six-inch pipe leading to the wheelhouse below.

There the helmsman controlled the ship's rudders and the lee helmsman operated the engine telegraph that told the engine room what speeds to maintain. Staying in line in daytime was seldom a problem because the helmsman could see the ship ahead and had only to be told to steer for it. Keeping interval was more complicated. If the second ship in column began to fall back, the third ship had to adjust its speed to compensate. Frequently number three would overcompensate, making life difficult for ship number four and the ships behind her. Station keeping at night was more complicated because the helmsman could not see the ship ahead. It became a stale joke for the OOD going off watch to quote Hamlet's Francisco: "For this relief, much thanks."

Sandy Hook vanished over the stern and the sea began to roll. Nothing violent, just enough to cause a queasy feeling. Most people feel motion sickness to some degree but hate to admit it. My own reaction was typical. No mad dash for the rail but rather an awareness that nausea could become a problem. On the second day out I had another awareness: hunger. That was soon attended to and it was smooth sailing thereafter. The crew adjusted to the day-and-a-half initiation period. Our bosun 2/c, a formidable young guy from Massachusetts, always carried a bucket on watch on his first day at sea after a long stay in port. No eyebrows were raised. Some crewmen were more severely stricken but the Navy would not recognize seasickness as a disabling condition. When our yeoman 1/c opened orders sending us to sea, he became ill immediately although we were still tied to the dock.

Mal de mer behind us, we soon adapted to seagoing life. The food wasn't bad. Chief Stevens did a credible job with powdered eggs, powdered milk, dried potatoes and frozen meat. The crew had their own names for the menu. Minced beef on toast became SOS (shit on a shingle); sliced baloney was horsecock. Unlike our Pacific LST brothers, we were seldom far from a supply base and fresh food. At sea, our freshwater showering was limited to a spray–soap–rinse routine. On long hauls, the fresh water was shut off and we could use all the salt water we wanted. Saltwater showers were tolerable. The water was warm and got you reasonably clean but it left a powdery residue that was hard to shed.

When John Neidermair designed the LST he obviously intended every square inch of space to be loaded with something. The bottom tanks (containers) were loaded with fuel and water. The tank deck was loaded with—what else?—tanks. The main deck was loaded with an LCT. Curious, I climbed onto the LCT and lifted its tarp. Sure enough, it was loaded with vegetables. On the ship's second deck, the narrow side compartments were lined with chain-supported pipe racks. Those intended for our passengers had four bunks to a rack. The top man's nose was seven inches from the overhead; the bottom man's bottom was four inches from the deck. No wonder the soldiers were always glad to get off the ship.

Three days out of New York, the sea was moderate and there were no U-Boat reports from the destroyer screen. If you could forget what lay ahead this was not a bad way to go. Our complacency didn't last. I suspected trouble when I saw both the engineering officer and his chief approaching the captain on the flag deck. Trouble with the starboard propeller shaft. "How much time to fix it," asked the captain. "Can't say," said the chief, "but I'll have to shut down the starboard engine right now." The skipper called up to the conning tower to stop the starboard engine. This cut our speed to about six knots. The ships astern began to pass us and soon we were dropping behind the convoy. The commodore sent a destroyer to cover us as we tried to repair the shaft. An hour dragged by and the convoy was disappearing over the horizon. One destroyer protecting one LST didn't make sense. The commodore ordered the destroyer back to the screen and spoke to us with his signal searchlight. "Head for Bermuda," he said. I believe he also wished us good luck. We needed it. An unprotected cargo ship traveling at six knots in the North Atlantic in 1943 was a sitting duck.

1943 North Atlantic Convoy (United States Government, public domain)

Up to this point our attempts at navigation had been interesting but not very important. We had known where we were. We were in position 4-6 in a Gibraltar-bound convoy. Now it was different. The convoy had vanished and we were alone on the open sea with orders to proceed to Bermuda. To find a heading for Bermuda I needed a starting point. I laid out a small-scale Atlantic chart and drew a straight line extending from New York, at 124 degrees (SE). We had advanced along that line 8.5 miles every hour we had traveled from Sandy Hook. I drew X at that point. From there I drew a line directly to Bermuda. The compass drawn on the chart told me that the new

German U-Boat (from Wikimedia Commons, public domain)

line was running south southwest (196 degrees). I called the new course up to the conning tower and crossed my fingers.

That kind of navigating is called dead reckoning and it works well under ideal conditions. What dead reckoning doesn't do is take into account the fact that winds and currents move the ship off of the straight line you just drew on the chart. There are no buoys or lighthouses on the high sea to tell you that you have strayed, but there are points of reference overhead: the sun, moon and stars. Rudimentary training at Princeton had acquainted me with a compass, sextant and nautical charts. On that meager basis I had brashly put myself forward as a navigator while we were still in Chesapeake Bay. I hadn't expected a real test this soon. We headed on our dead reckoning line to Bermuda and I broke out the sextant and started shooting sun lines. That is, I measured the angle the sun made with the horizon. With that angle applied to Greenwich Time of day, I was able to draw a line on the chart. We were somewhere on that line. In the evening I used a bright star to plot a similar line. Our ship was located somewhere near the point where the two lines crossed. We called that point a "fix." That technique is called "celestial navigation" and it involves spherical trigonometry—something I wasn't particularly good at. But back in the time of the Revolutionary War, a man named Nathaniel Bowditch put the whole matter in tabular form for amateurs like me.

We plugged along for two days, our eyes alert for U-Boats. We even doubled the lookouts even though U-Boats didn't usually approach their targets on the surface. In the middle of the third day we saw Bermuda. Nobody shouted "Land Ho" Columbus style, but we sure shouted—the rookie navigator loudest of all.

Back to complacency. Bermuda lived up to its reputation of broad beaches and ocean views. We weren't particularly interested in ocean views at the time. In the best nautical tradition we came ashore looking for girls and barrooms. The barrooms were easy to find, but Bermuda had a population of only about 50,000 at the time and the few girls were well attended by the local population and the personnel at the navy base. Bermuda's

State House in St. George's, Bermuda *(from Wikimedia Commons 3.0)*

Beach in Bermuda *(© Ministry of Tourism and Transport, Bermuda, with permission)*

appeal to this crypto-Luddite lay in the absence of internal combustion engines. There wasn't a car on the island outside the navy base. Our ship motor machinists (black gang) were hard at work on the propeller shaft but the rest of us were free to roam the island in horse-drawn carriages and on bicycles. Wandering about those blissful surroundings it was hard to realize that the world was falling apart all around us. Bermuda was a nice place to spend the war and our crew didn't hesitate to let the base personnel know how they felt about it. Fred Chatterton, my lawyer shipmate, asked the OOD at the base for transportation to a point apparently out of bounds.

"If I did that, I might get shipped out," said the OOD.

Fred was caustic. "Now we wouldn't want that to happen, would we?"

The shaft was fixed and our idyll ended. We bid Circe goodbye and joined a passing convoy. The run to Gibraltar was uneventful. We passed near, but out of sight of, the Azores. I thought it would be great to spend a week there comparing those islands with Bermuda, but we sailed on. I later learned that LST 228 ran—or was blown—aground there the following winter. It was one of the many losses the LST fleet suffered in the European Theater of Operations. We closed on North Africa and soon we could smell the land. I hadn't anticipated the differences between sea breezes and those that had blown over forest, plains and rivers.

The Straits of Gibraltar are less than 20 miles across. We could admire the famous Rock as we passed through, but we were more concerned with the fact that this concentration of Allied shipping provided the best hunting ground the U-Boats could hope for. Fortunately, the Allies had the world's best anti-sub devices in place there. We passed through without incident and proceeded through the Mediterranean Sea to our first oversea port, a little town on the Morocco–Algeria border called Nemours, a name I can't find on my 1986 atlas.

Our convoy dispersed; some LSTs moored in local harbors, and others continued east toward the action. The Allies had

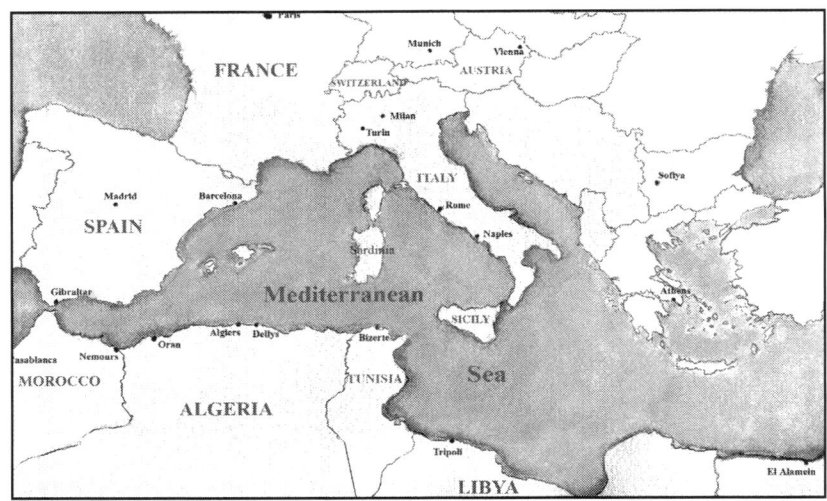

Mediterranean Sea

Rock of Gibraltar (from Wikimedia Commons, public domain)

only recently driven Rommel out of North Africa. Our stay in Nemours was brief, and a few days later we were anchored at Mers el Kebir on the west shore of Oran Harbor. There we met the enemy. The signal tower sent a Red Alert just before midnight. We sounded the general alarm (General Quarters in ship talk) and for the first time our youthful crew ran to their battle stations ready to shoot. There wasn't much to shoot at. The bombers were there alright, the searchlights held them in their beams, but they were so high we could hardly see them. Our 20 mm's were outranged but we did have the 3"/50 mounted on our stern and we fired away with that. The gun crew did well. The pointer and trainer stayed on target and the loaders kept the shells moving. Only the "hot shell" man had trouble. His job was to clear the ejected shell casings from the deck, but whatever training he had did not include night work. The loaders did their job while stumbling over empty casings in the dark. The bombers didn't hit any ships and the ships didn't hit any bombers. The first round was a draw.

We moved east from Oran to a place called Arzew where we gave a demonstration of LST versatility. We had been carrying the 900-ton LCT on our back since March and we were anxious to get rid of it. A special LST feature came into play here. Our bottom tanks could be flooded or voided readily. That gave us control of the ship's draft for deep sea cruising or for shallow beach landings. It also gave us control over our port and starboard tilt, or list. In Arzew harbor we voided our port tanks creating a 16 degree list to starboard. We then cut a cable and the LCT slid along its greased supporting beams and went gracefully over the side. It hit the water with a great splash and then surged back against the ship. We were prepared for that. Large woven cane fenders were strung along the ship's side and they absorbed the recoil. Mission accomplished. We were 900 tons lighter and, with the LCT crew gone, had six fewer mouths to feed.

We moved east along the North African coast, always careful to stay close to shore. And with good reason. On June 22, one of our group, LST 333, was torpedoed by a U-Boat about

LST 318 Launching an LCT (National Archives: NH 84848)

200 miles east of Arzew. With the help of other ships in the convoy, the skipper was able to beach his ship near a town called Dellys. Twenty-five dead.

We passed Dellys a few days before LST 333 was hit and put into crowded Bizerte harbor. We expected to take on a load of the Sherman tanks we were designed to handle. Instead we took on a load of trucks loaded with ammunition. Eleven of those trucks were DUKWs, seagoing trucks with a watertight hull and a propeller. DUKWs were very useful when the sea was calm but easily swamped when it was rough. Ordered to leave Bizerte harbor, we sailed around a point of land into the Bay of Tunis to a small harbor called La Goulette near Carthage. We were now only 125 miles from the enemy at Marsala, Sicily. On July 1 our ship's log had the routine entry:

> *0800-1200 Anchored in Tunis Bay with 56 fathoms (336') of chain to the bow anchor in 3 1/2 fathoms of water on the following bearings: St Louis Chapel 005", Rades 254', Jebel bu Kurnin 166'.*

I'm not too sure of that last spelling. The handwriting isn't very clear. The log was signed by Gene Jaeger, Ensign, USNR.

The Luftwaffe didn't bother us much at La Goulette but we could watch their nightly attacks on Bizerte, 15 miles to the northwest. We were alerted to defend ourselves against "limpet"

LST 333 struck in stern by torpedo launched by U-Boat (United States Government, public domain)

attacks in which a bomb with a suction device was attached to the hull of the ship by an underwater swimmer. Italian frogmen had made several successful limpet attacks at Gibraltar the previous year. Our defense was a boat patrol with the crew dropping explosives to discourage underwater swimming.

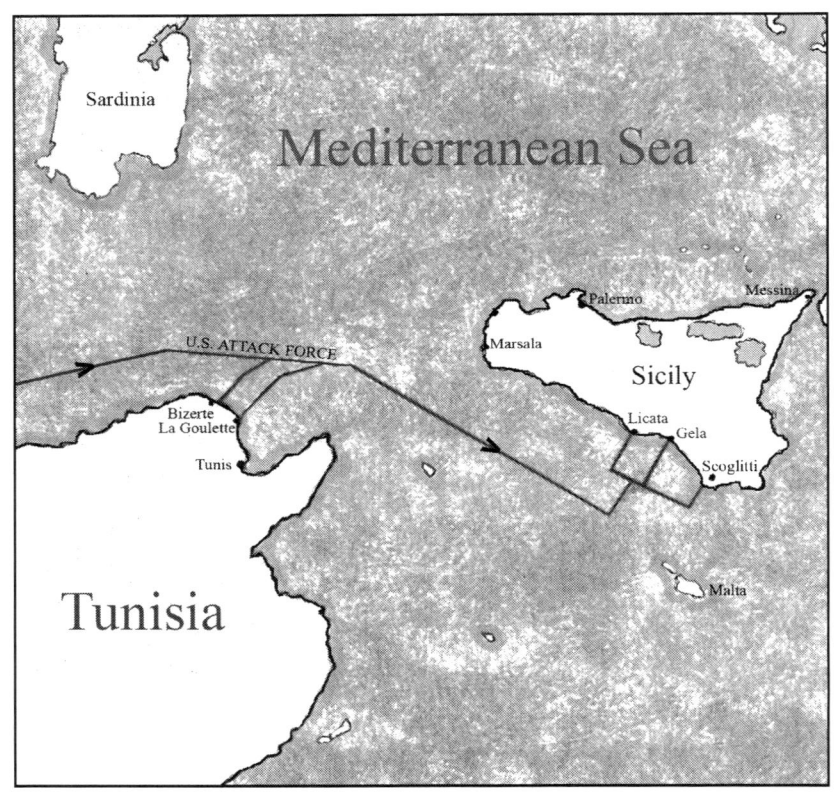

U.S. Attack Force on Sicily

Chapter 3

Sicily

The U.S. Army Air Force carried out massive daylight bombings of Schweinfurt and Regensburg in mid-1943. The U.S. Army recaptured Attu in the Aleutians and New Georgia in the Solomon Islands in June.

July 8, 1943 was a calm, sunny day. That had been the Mediterranean pattern for the past month. The Luftwaffe had made a pass at us the night before. They knew what was about to happen as well as we did. We had our written orders: target Sicily. Chaplains of all denominations visited the ship. The Catholic chaplain gave the faithful general absolution.

At 5:48 AM we hauled in the anchor and headed north out of the Bay of Tunis to join an eastbound convoy carrying the vanguard of the Seventh Army under General George S. Patton. The convoy was in order. The destroyer screen was in place; troopships and cargo ships were in column and the smaller landing craft struggled to keep up. I took a long look at the rising sun, dead ahead. I also had time to admire a recent acquisition called a barrage balloon. This silver blimp was attached to our fore rail by a 500 foot, ¾" wire cable. An explosive canister, about the size of a two-pound coffee can, was attached about half way up the cable. This was intended to ward off low flying bombers and torpedo planes. Combat utility aside, the barrage balloons did give the convoy a festive air.

We drove east, ever on the lookout for enemy planes. U-Boats were the escort's problem. About 5:00 PM on July 9

Head-On Sea (National Archives: 80-G-65893)

Bob Brown, S2/c (courtesy of the family of Bob Brown)

LST with Barrage Balloon (National Archives: SC 190462)

our attack force wheeled left and headed north for the town of Gela on Sicily's south shore. If the Axis brass had any doubts as to where we were heading, they knew for sure at this point. About this time the light breeze stiffened and we saw low clouds on the horizon on our port bow. The Mediterranean dropped its friendly façade and we soon had a full gale pounding on our bow. LSTs had a tough time with a heading sea. Their flat bottoms held them high on the crest of each wave from which they slid down into the trough to meet the oncoming wave head on, not knifing through it like a destroyer or cruiser, but rather slamming the blunt bow into it with a crash that made the whole ship shudder. Later in the war we cracked our main deck from side to side in such a storm. The captain commented on the storm in his action report:

> *By 6:55 PM wind had increased to strength seven and by using full rudder and wide changes in engine speeds was able to maintain course within ten degrees to either side. At 7:09 PM the wind carried away the barrage balloon and the explosive charge fell into the landing boat, but, fortunately, did not detonate. About the same time the port screw (propeller) came out of the water and the overspeed trip stopped the engine making steering virtually impossible till the engine was started again. Soon after darkness the sea gradually subsided and station keeping became a possibility instead of a desire.*

Along with his other accomplishments, the captain could turn a colorful phrase.

It's easy for me to remember the barrage balloon incident. I was standing on the port bridge wing about ten feet forward of the landing boat watching the balloon veer violently from side to side. The cable snapped, the balloon headed for the stratosphere and the canister came flying aft, right at me. I dove behind a gun mount just as the canister whacked the bottom of the boat. No explosion! The charge must have been deactivated—or was it? While I pondered the situation a bold young seaman, I think it was Bob Brown, climbed up into the boat and threw the damned thing over the side.

The convoy was shaken, but still holding together. The wind eased at nightfall but low clouds held visibility to a minimum. Each ship had a small, blue light mounted on its stern to guide the following ship. Not quite good enough. The first light of morning on July 10 showed us to be almost alone. The LST ahead of us was following another LST which was following—nothing. The three of us were running unescorted well within enemy waters. For several hours we had been seeing red flashes on the bottom of the cloud cover to the northwest, presumably gunfire. The captain left our wayward guide and pointed our bow at the red flashes. Soon we could see the invasion fleet, about five miles off our port bow. At full daylight on the morning of July 10 we were hove to (stopped but not anchored) in the staging area, two hours behind schedule. The plan called for us to join the command ship, USS *Barnett*, at which point we were to launch our DUKWs. The *Barnett* was nowhere in sight. We could have searched for it but our real objective was to place ammunition on Red Beach One. We dropped the stern anchor, opened the bow doors and lowered the ramp. Eleven DUKWs rolled down the ramp, into the sea and headed for the beach, shepherded by our young Texan, Ensign Krezdorn, in one of our landing boats. This was the first use of DUKWs in amphibious warfare. I wonder what the troops on the beach felt when they saw what appeared to be low-slung, overloaded boats hit the shore, pause, and then waddle slowly out of the water, across the sandy beach, and disappear down the road.

We weighed anchor and moved to a point about 1,000 yards off Red Beach One where we waited for a pontoon bridge to become available. The LSTs were grounding well offshore. This was anticipated and several LSTs carried pontoon bridge sections lashed to their sides. LSTs could carry anything. The pontoon sections were maneuvered to the beach and formed into bridges extending out to the point where the LSTs were grounding. The LSTs laid their bow ramps on the seaward end of the bridge and

DUKW Making a Landing (National Archives: 80-G-252737)

the tanks rolled ashore. This engineering work was done under fire. German tanks were working in the area and the beach was being bombed by low flying Me109s that flew down river valleys to the shoreline where a right angle turn sent them streaking over the beach at very low altitudes. They were on us before we could react. We fired our 20 mm's and 40 mm's at those speedy targets. No hits.

War has little aesthetic appeal. Amphibious landings, in particular, turn a beautiful shoreline into a junkyard in less than an hour. But on July 10 I saw a battle scene that was a work of art—lethal but beautiful. Enemy tanks had broken through on our right flank and had the exposed landing craft in enfilade. We could hear them calling for help on the radios. They got it. I looked aft to see a light cruiser, I believe it was the USS *Savannah*, coming up fast on our starboard quarter. She headed for the beach with a bone in her teeth (Navy talk for a roll of white water at the bow of a speeding ship). The cruiser held fire until she was about 1,000 yards offshore where she put her helm hard over for a right turn. The high speed turn heeled the ship sharply to port, putting her guns temporarily out of action. The ship slowly righted itself as it came broadside to the beach and its six-inch guns came on target. They all fired at once, putting the first salvo right on target. The tanks disappeared in a cloud of gun smoke and were seen no more.

While we waited for our pontoon bridge to become available the battle continued on land, on the sea and in the air. High flying Fw200s continued to attack throughout the afternoon of July 10. I don't recall firing our 3" rifle at them. About 6:30 PM we opened fire with our 20s and 40s at an Me109 making a run at Red Beach One. We should have hit it. The sonofabitch scored a direct hit on our group mate, LST 313, and set it on fire. The stage was set for another movie-style drama. The 313 and LST 311 were unloading side by side over separate pontoon bridges when the bomb struck. The 311 had finished unloading and was hauling in on her stern anchor cable and slowly drawing off the beach. With what seemed to me a remarkable bit of seamanship, the skipper of the 311 stopped retracting and moved back toward the beach laying his starboard bow against the port quarter of the burning 313 and held it there while some of the 313 crew scrambled to safety. That 64-year-old scene was brought back to me on the bridge deck of LST 325 in Peoria in 2007. I was sitting on a ready-box in front of the wheelhouse with my granddaughter when an old guy approached wearing a blue baseball cap with a gold insignia: USS LST 313. "Red Beach One?" I asked. He thought about it for a while. "I was on the 313 at Gela," he replied. Of course, he wouldn't remember the beach name. I only knew it because I'd been writing about it the night before. The old sailor's name is Sam Nauyalis and he lives in the village of Spring Valley on the north shore of the Illinois River about 50 miles upstream from Peoria. Sam was a Motor Machinist's Mate 2/c on LST 313 when it was bombed. Here's his story.

> *In the afternoon we moved into the beach. My battle station was in the engine room with three other guys. We grounded on a sandbar about two-hundred feet offshore and the bridge*

USS **Savannah** *(National Archives: NH 97956)*

LST 325 off-loading on a Pontoon Bridge *(U.S. Government, public domain)*

LST 313 burning after being hit by a German bomber, July, 1943 (U.S. Army, public domain)

On September 1, 2007, survivor Sam Nauyalis tells Gene Jaeger and granddaughter Reilly of his escape from the burning LST 313. (courtesy of the author)

called down for full power and all engines were running when it hit. There was a loud thump and all the asbestos flew off the pipes. There was no smoke or flame in the engine room but the bridge called for all engines stopped, and then ABANDON SHIP. We headed for the exit shaft and I was the last one up the ladder. Out on deck I started forward toward the beach but my way was blocked by flame and smoke amidships. I knew the tank deck was loaded with gasoline and ammunition so I headed back to the stern and off to starboard I saw an LCM (landing craft, medium) trying to pick up men in the water. I decided to head for it but I didn't want to jump 20 feet from the main deck so I slid down the stern anchor cable. I inflated my Mae West (life preserver) before I hit the water and started paddling for the LCM. It was bobbing up and down and I was afraid to get too close to it. Then I saw that LST 311 had put its bow up against our stern and I headed for it. When I got alongside, the crew lowered a line. I didn't have enough strength left to climb it. I knew all the Navy knots so I tied the line around me and the crew hoisted me up to the main deck. The 311 took me back to La Goulette. The Chateau Thierry *took me to Mers el Kebir where I was shipped back to the States to pick up another LST.*

The bombing of LST 313 wasn't the end of the war for Sam. He picked up a new LST in the States and was back in time for a D-Day landing at Omaha Beach in Normandy. From there he went to Naples to pick up a load for the invasion of southern France. Sam Nauyalis finished the war as a Chief Motor Machinist on the beaches of Japan.

The loss of a pontoon bridge changed our plans and we started unloading the ammunition trucks into shallow draft landing craft. Shortly after sunset LCT 196 moored bow-to-bow with us—"married" in our new jargon. The trucks began to roll from our tank deck to theirs. They were able to beach without the pontoons and they were back in three hours for another load. We were still unloading onto LCT 196 the next morning, July 11, when we were attacked by another flight of the high-level Fw200s. We escaped damage but the USS *Barnett* was hit and set

Me109 (from Wikimedia Commons 2.0)

Fw200 (from Bundesarchiv, Wikimedia Commons 3.0)

LST 158 burning on a beach at Licata (National Archives: SC 489601)

afire. They put out the fire but they lost seven men. Several ships in our group claimed to have hit one of the attacking planes, but I didn't see any fall. Other beaches were under artillery fire and aerial bombardment. LST 158 was hit while unloading on a beach just east of Licata. I have a letter from Joe LePage, of Redding, CA, describing that action. Joe was on LST 376 and had a clear view of the bombing. He wrote:

> ...we were ½ to ¾ miles off the coast and the 158 was beached. We were at general quarters and I was pointer on a 20 mm. I observed an Me109 diving at an almost 90° angle at the 158 and he let go a bomb that hit it.
>
> The LST gunners hit the plane which I believe was traveling at least 400 M.P.H. It crashed in the water to port of the 158 which had its nose on the beach. I hardly saw any wreckage of the plane when it hit the ocean but I saw a large oil slick. Do not know if this is only scuttlebutt (rumor) or not but heard afterwards that some of ship's company had real serious injuries from jumping into the ocean with their helmets strapped under their necks.
>
> Hoping this will help you out...Joe LePage

We'll hear more from Joe in the Normandy invasion.

By 4:30 PM on the 11th we had unloaded all army personnel and materials and separated from our "mate" LCT 196. We anchored out of range of shore guns but the air war continued. At 5:00 PM a merchant ship, unloading near Licata, was bombed and set afire. It was apparently loaded with ammunition. When it exploded half an hour later it sent a column of smoke a mile into the sky. The blast set fire to nearby ships. I welcomed the cover of darkness but I hadn't reckoned on magnesium flares. At 10:00 PM an unseen plane laid out three flares, each floating downward in its little parachute and lighting up the sky like Times Square. I could see every ship in the invasion fleet and so could the bombers. With their target illuminated, the Fw200s came at us out of the southeast again. None of their bombs fell close to us but then—tragedy struck. The next episode was one of those grotesque nightmares that are as much a part of war as Arlington Cemetery. The Fw's were overhead, the Me's had just left the beach. The sky was filled with the red tails of our anti-aircraft tracers when a new flight of planes entered the scene approaching from the southwest—from North Africa. They were flying low and dropping flares as they came. But the flares weren't for illumination, they were recognition flares but nobody recognized them. The trigger-happy invasion fleet opened fire on them with immediate success. Many of the intruders began to fall and burn. Then a few of our gunners began to realize that these were not German bombers; they were cargo planes, our own C47s. And their cargo, God help us, was our own paratroops. I don't know how many planes we shot down. We didn't know the full extent of the catastrophe until we saw our own airborne soldiers floating face down in Gela Bay the next morning. The LST crews weren't the only ones getting on-the-job training at Sicily that night. I'll bet our military planners never again sent airborne troop carriers flying low over an embattled invasion fleet.

At 10 AM on the morning of July 12 we were bound for Bizerte for another load. I don't recall our cargo for the follow-up landing. We were still working with General Patton's Seventh Army and we could have been hauling tanks, half-tracks and ammunition or it could have been food, fuel or any of the miscellany that modern (1943) armies traveled with. A deckhand told me that he had personally unloaded a folding canvas bathtub intended for the general himself. Strange cargo for a fighting ship but, as I say, LSTs carry anything. We were leaving the dock in Bizerte when a bosun came to me with a story of even stranger cargo. One of the trucks on the tank deck had a dead cow lying under its tarp. How the hell did that happen? As the bosun told it, the Sicily-bound GIs were having a final party at a rundown pub in a small Tunisian town. A soldier suggested that they do something for their buddies who were already on the front line.

As the night wore on there was a growing conviction that what their buddies needed was fresh meat. They drove to a peasant's farm, killed a cow, loaded it on a truck and had it aboard our ship early the next day. The bosun was insulted that anybody would think they could bring dead livestock aboard his ship.

"How did they kill the cow," I asked.

"With a submachine gun," he replied, "what should I do about it."

I was a very young officer to be faced with decisions like that, but I met it head-on.

"Ignore it."

One effort to alleviate the austerity of shipboard life was the V Disc, an outsized version of the standard 78 rpm phonograph record of the time. Popular artists recorded on V Discs, gratis I believe. Our record player was located in the wardroom from where the music could be piped throughout the ship, including a loudspeaker mounted just forward of the bridge. Wardroom personnel could select the music and direct it to any part of the ship. On one of our Sicily landings we were threatened by counterattacking Italian troops and tension built as we neared the beach. At the moment the skipper called out "let go the stern anchor" a switch was flipped in the wardroom and we hit the sand with Patty, LaVerne and Maxine Andrews blasting out "The Pennsylvania Polka." I can only guess at the effect *that* had on the defenders.

When the crew was at battle stations the wardroom pantry was manned by a black crewman. The three blacks in our crew were servants. The United States was segregated throughout World War II and blacks in the military were treated the same as they were in civilian life. I knew only a few blacks in small town mid-America while I was growing up. I expected them to always be dressed in work clothes and doing menial jobs. That was the world I saw and nobody in my family, my church or my schools had ever told me different. So it seemed quite normal in the Navy to find these young men sweeping my cabin, making my bed and serving the food in the wardroom. But something positive did happen. When we went to battle stations one of the blacks (we called them mess boys) was stationed in the wardroom pantry, seeing that coffee and sandwiches were available. The other two were assigned to gun crews and when the German planes came at us, black and white gunners stood shoulder to shoulder firing at a common enemy. I don't pretend that an epiphany occurred; segregation continued in force. But what was happening on our ship was happening throughout the armed forces. It's just possible that those occasional moments of shared humanity made us a little more receptive to the message of the black leaders of the fifties.

On our third trip we rounded the southeast tip of Sicily and sailed into Syracuse harbor with a payload for General Montgomery who was working his way up the east coast of the island toward Messina while General Patton was approaching the city from the west. With several Sicilian port cities now in our hands it was no longer necessary for us to unload on the beaches. We waited in Syracuse for an open dock. It was an uneasy night. We spent most of it at battle stations alternately firing at the Luftwaffe or admiring the red glow of Mt. Etna, 40 miles to the north. Bombs fell from time to time and our searchlights were picking up the attackers directly overhead. We were firing the new anti-aircraft shells, set to detonate when they reached a pre-set altitude. The shrapnel fell back down on us, clanking as it hit the steel deck. Nobody was hit but we kept our steel helmets on throughout the night.

In his move on Messina, Patton used amphibious end runs to flank the enemy on Sicily's north shore. LST 318 was sunk on one of those raids. The Allies continued to pour a steady flow of men and arms onto the island and soon had enough power to drive the German and Italian forces back. A great deal has been made of Generals Montgomery and Patton racing to take Messina. They both lost. On August 17, nearly 100,000 Axis troops with their vehicles escaped across the Straits of Messina to the Italian mainland.

All military operations are subject to endless review and evaluation by military chiefs, scholars, journalists and the guy at the end of the bar. Our review came from our captain in a mandatory report to his flotilla commander.

Personnel

Considering the fact that ninety percent of the ship's company had never been under fire before I consider the way that the great majority conducted themselves was a fine tribute to the spirit of our manhood. No confusion or terror was apparent in their first baptism of war.

Training

Prior to the time that the gun's crews started firing for their lives they never had an opportunity to fire their guns at a target. They had received a woefully small amount of training at various gunnery schools that partially equipped them to meet very commonplace problems.

Gunners had received virtually no training in use of a MK14 sight and habitually used tracer Control in place of the site (sic). Prior to 7 July 1943 the ship had not been able to obtain an adequate supply of axis and allied plane character sheets for proper training. A "hurry up" school was started when these sheets were obtained and with the assistance of RAF personnel aboard the men were given a fair course in the identification of the more common types.

Material

Faulty primers in 20MM ammunition caused a few jams, but less than test firing had led us to suspect. No trouble was experienced with the 40MM guns or 3"/50. Remainder of the ship's equipment operated satisfactorily with the exception of fuel oil lines (see log).

Recommendations

Aircraft identification sheets be made available to ships PRIOR to leaving the States so that a proper training schedule can be instituted. Gun crews be given opportunities to fire on moving targets with their ship's guns. If they are given equipment such as Mark 14 sights to use they should be given numerous opportunities to use them on HIGH SPEED TARGETS.

Not a bad report card. Apparently the captain's opinion was that although the crew was poorly trained, they *did* put the army ashore at the assigned beach in spite of everything the enemy and the weather could do to stop them.

Chapter 4

After the Battle

In combat zones, the crew was in a constant state of readiness. Out of range of shore batteries and minefields, shipboard life was still highly organized and confining but not unpleasant.

Sicily was ours. Like their great-grandfathers in the Civil War, the crew had seen the elephant. Going into our first battle we knew that modern weapons would kill a lot of men. We knew it like we knew that while all John Wayne's victims were dead, that somehow they would show up in another movie at another time. Not this time. The men on LST 313 and in the C47s were

Shipmates Aboard LST 400: *Looks like a high school basketball team. Actually these youngsters had two invasions behind them at the time this picture was taken. (courtesy of the author)*

dead, really dead. And the crew knew that there was more of this harsh reality to come. But they had faced the monster once and they knew they could do it again. They were no longer 18-year-old kids; they were 18-year-old men.

Battle experience was only part of the change. In the past six months the crew had learned to live in its 328' x 50' steel cocoon. It was a life that lacked peacetime comforts but it sure beat hell out of sleeping in a foxhole on a cold rainy night. The first thing to get used to was lack of privacy. There was always someone within six feet of you. This could be a comfort at times; it could also be a pain in the ass. The deck, bulkhead and overhead (floor, walls and ceiling) were painted shades of gray and blue but I never found that depressing. I could always step out on the open deck to behold the sea and sky or a crowded harbor. Long treks on the open sea could be a bore but I always enjoyed sailing within sight of the ever-changing shoreline.

Then there was the day-to-day routine. A rigid shipboard schedule sounds oppressive, and it can be. But given the fact that our choice of activities was limited by our confinement, the schedule did have the advantage of answering that plaguing question: What do I do now? In port or at sea, the official day began with an 8:00 AM muster of all hands on the main deck. The colors were raised, roll was called and occasionally announcements were made. This was followed by calisthenics, a routine performance but sometimes quite colorful at sea. One exercise, called "jumping jacks," if done in a rolling sea was fascinating to watch. It began with your feet together and your arms at your sides. The next move is a jump to a straddle position with your hands meeting over your head. While the jump took your feet momentarily off the deck, the rolling ship moved beneath them so that you landed an inch or so from where you took off. As a result, the crew jumping in unison moved slowly across the deck to the port rail, and then, as the ship righted itself, they bounced slowly back to starboard. Watching this performance from the bridge you had the feeling that, in a prolonged roll, the crew would dance right over the side and into the ocean.

LST Rolling in a Moderate Sea (U.S. Government, public domain)

After muster, in port, each crewman went to work on his own specialty. In Navy talk, he "turned to." The gunner's mates cleaned and oiled guns; machinists did the same with the ship's machinery. I could list the activities of our 100-man crew, but I'd rather stick to the routine of the crewman I knew best: me.

Like the rest of the crew, I had in-port and at-sea routines. In-port was less demanding. After the 8:00 AM muster, my first stop was the radio shack. There the radioman sat at his typewriter, headphones in place, facing his gauges and dials. I read everything he logged since my last visit. Some of the messages were routine, some routed immediately to the captain, some held navigational data: lighthouse out of action, ship sunk in the fairway, missing buoy (possibly run down by an LST). A few messages had to be decoded. My job.

My next stop was the chart room where the quartermaster stood ready to enter on his charts any changes I brought from the radio shack. Next, the chronometer. This was a very special clock mounted in gimbal rings to keep it as level as possible when the ship was rolling. The chronometer kept Greenwich Mean Time (GMT) which is to say the time kept at the Royal Observatory at Greenwich (pronounced gren' itch) on the south bank of the Thames River downstream from London. The Observatory stands at 0 degrees longitude, the Prime Meridian. It is from this point that longitude is measured to the west and to the east. GMT is essential to navigation out of sight of land. Every day, at a given hour, naval observatories throughout the world send a radio signal marking Greenwich time.

Next, up to the flag deck where signalmen kept their eyes on the flagship, the shore station or other ships. They were watching for flag or blinker signals. The signal flags were three-foot squares of durable cloth, light enough to stand out in a moderate breeze. Each flag had a special design and was named for a letter in the alphabet. When fixed to a halyard (clothesline) in groups of four and hoisted to a yardarm, the flags had special messages: "close up," "stand by for a turn to port," "go to battle stations." Blinker signals were sent by a two-foot diameter, shuttered searchlight. The shutters were opened and closed by a side lever with which the signalman sent Morse Code dots and dashes. Each letter of the alphabet had a special name: A=Able, B=Baker, C=Charlie. This prevented confusing the sound-alike letters, such as B, G, E, P. A few messages were delivered in person. These were the ones marked Restricted, Secret or Top Secret.

Finally, I'd reach the conning tower. Not much of a tower really, only a few feet above the flag deck and measuring about six by six with a four-foot bulkhead. There wasn't much to do in the conning tower while the ship was in port unless you happened to be the officer-of-the-deck. Then you'd probably scan the harbor, see how the anchor chain was riding and generally overlook activities on the main deck.

The in-port OOD oversaw the ship's routine for twenty-four hours but was able to lead a fairly normal life. He spent most of his time at the gangway (ladder reaching down to the dock or the water's edge) monitoring the comings and goings of the crew. If the ship was anchored out, he managed the boats. LSTs carried 36-foot landing boats called LCVPs (Landing Craft, Vehicles and Personnel). These boats seemed to take on different names depending on the job they were doing at the time. Headed for the beach they were true landing craft, but headed for the Fleet Post Office, they were mail boats. If they carried off-duty sailors for a night on the town, they were liberty boats. And that's only a few of the LCVP's functions.

Life at sea was a more strenuous routine. The OOD kept station in the convoy, passing orders from the conning tower to the wheelhouse below. The conversation usually sounded like this:

OOD: "Right ten degrees rudder."

Helmsman: "Right ten degrees rudder, sir."

Pause

Helmsman: "The rudder is ten degrees right, sir."

OOD: "Very well."

Or, if adjustments in speed were required, the exchange would sound like this:

OOD: "Starboard engine ahead two-thirds."

Lee Helmsman: "Starboard engine ahead two-thirds, sir."

This would be followed by the ringing sound of the engine telegraph's signal followed by the ringing sound of the engine room's reply.

Lee Helmsman: "The starboard engine *is* ahead two-thirds, sir."

OOD: "Very well."

The OOD also had a speaking tube leading to the captain's cabin. The skipper insisted on being notified of significant changes while the ship was underway. We didn't always see eye-to-eye on what was significant. I can recall a few occasions on which the captain read the night log and then called the OOD to account: "Why didn't you call me?"

About fifteen minutes before the end of each sea watch, messengers were sent below to alert the relief watch. Showing up late for your watch was not punishable by court martial, but the wounded look from your weary shipmate could be just as bad. Before the OOD could leave the bridge he was required to write the deck log covering his time on watch. Log entries included changes in course, speed, sighting of other ships or landmarks plus other occurrences. That finished, the OOD had eight hours before his next watch. Time for division duties as well as sleeping and eating.

Feeding 100 young men three times a day was a major factor. Chief Commissary Steward (head cook) Stevens had about ten years' regular navy time under his belt and he knew his way around. There were times he'd return from the supply depot with a load of frozen beef when other ships in our flotilla hadn't seen beef for weeks. There were rumors that the chief had a deal with the pharmacist's mate and, when the occasion required, he could lay hands on a half-gallon of alcohol as a bargaining chip. He never told us; we never asked. By 1943, food manufacturers had developed drying processes that supplied us with powdered eggs, milk and potatoes and powdered God-knows-what. The process made passable scrambled eggs, but I never was able to use powdered milk on my cornflakes. Of course, the crew griped about the food, usually good-naturedly. An Italian cook from St. Louis prepared beans that were somewhat on the solid side. The crew called them Bellini's bullets, but they ate them. The crew loaded their trays in the galley and carried them down one deck to the mess hall. Officers had their meals served by white-jacketed mess boys in the wardroom, but it all came out of the same pot.

Chief Stevens inspected the food carefully before accepting it from the supply base but in one incident, I don't know if he was watching out for our health or for his own particular taste. We were told to prepare for a load of trucks and 200 troops on a follow-up landing. The commissary sent over a load of liver to feed the GIs (a helluva thing to feed men going into battle). The trucks arrived, but the troops got hung up and we sailed without them. No troops, but plenty of liver. We were barely out of

LST Galley (courtesy of CB&I)

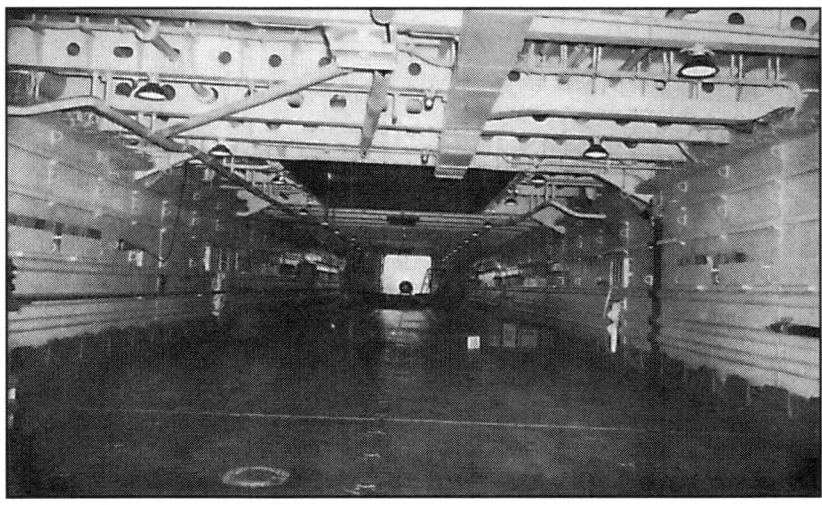

LST Tank Deck, Looking out through Bow Doors (courtesy of CB&I)

sight of land when the chief came up to the bridge to tell me that he couldn't fit the liver into the crew's menu for a few days and that it would soon spoil. He needed the OOD's permission to jettison the load. He got it readily. I didn't like liver any more than he did.

Sleeping arrangements were adequate. Sailors traveled with sea bags which supposedly carried everything they needed, including a mattress. They spread their mattresses on a canvas base, stretched tautly on a pipe rack. Crew's quarters were well ventilated, although I've heard horror stories about the ventilation on troopships. Once a week, if the sea was calm, the bosun would pipe "air bedding" at which the crew would carry their bedding aloft and hang it over the ship's rail for an hour.

In spite of the overloads of men and materials, LSTs were kept very clean. We had plenty of men to do the job. A peacetime cargo ship of our size would probably carry a crew of 30 men. We needed 100 men to man all guns and stations at General Quarters. When not manning guns there were plenty of men to scrub deck, chip paint and clean quarters. I'm told that the "white glove" navy (carriers, cruisers, battleships) carried cleanliness to the extreme in the form of frequent inspections in which an officer wearing white gloves would run his fingers along the top of a hatch looking for dust. We didn't go that far. In fact, after a few weeks at sea we dropped inspections altogether. But we did keep a clean ship.

We were comfortably and functionally clothed. Ninety percent of the time I was on LST 400 the crew wore denim and the officers wore khaki. Our electrically-operated laundry was more than adequate. We had no trouble with personal cleanliness. The only sailor who fell short in that department was put straight by shipmates, not officers. Ashore, men wore blues or whites; officers wore blues or khakis. There was such a thing as officer's dress whites but I don't recall seeing them in the Med or in London. I didn't own a set. We were well-protected in cold and wet weather with fur-lined coveralls, jackets and caps.

Our fleece lined, mitten-like gloves had a detached trigger finger. For wet weather we had the traditional oilskins, officially known as "foul weather gear," a catching phrase. I heard an ensign who had been struck in the groin by a throwing line refer to the damaged area as his foul weather gear.

There were plenty of showers for the crew but none for our soldier passengers who usually spent only one night aboard. Water was a problem only when we had been several days at sea. When the freshwater tanks ran down we switched to saltwater showers. They got us clean enough, but they left an unpleasant salty residue.

There was little leisure at sea. Gambling was permitted but I don't recall any high-roller games. Much of the free time was spent writing letters. This put a drag on the officers' free time. We had to censor outgoing mail, usually about two-hundred letters a week. At first we took this seriously. But as months went by and no military secrets were being revealed, we took to scanning the letter briefly before stamping them CENSORED. I believe some of the officers quit reading them altogether. If you did that you could stamp and seal 40 letters in a few minutes.

Incoming mail though was a serious matter, the high spot of the week. The mail was picked up and distributed by an exuberant young seaman from upstate Vermont who rose from his routine duties as a deckhand to the eminence of mail clerk. The crew's hunger for letters from home was such that at mail call the clerk's standing aboard ship was nearly equal to that of the captain. For a few hours, the ship was his. The first step after anchoring in a new port was the lowering of an LCVP, now the *mail boat*. It took the clerk to the fleet post office. If all went well with Navy postal service, he returned with a sack of mail. The clerk and the mail sack were paraded down the ladder to the crew's quarters where he mounted a mess table and began to read off names and flip the letters to outstretched hands. For some reason he'd guffaw loudly when he identified the sender as a girlfriend. I once watched him doling out mail to the off-duty crew. An impatient seaman had the temerity to thumb through a packet of mail lying on the table. The mail clerk eyed him coldly: "Keep your filthy fuckin' fingers off the mail." That blast of contemptuous alliteration hasn't been matched in my lifetime. Mail call ended on a gray note for those who walked away empty-handed.

The relationship between officers and men varied from ship to ship depending on the demeanor of the commanding officer. On LST 400 formalities were kept to a minimum, just enough to maintain the military line of authority. Officers were always called mister but almost never saluted. At the outset the crew was told that it would be necessary only to salute officers at the first meeting of the day. Even that casual greeting faded away after a few months and soon only the captain was so greeted. I've seen movies where an enlisted man, when addressed by an officer, would snap to attention and shout: "Sir, yes sir." Not in my navy. That we kept to military discipline without the harsh regimen was due, I think, to the demeanor of our skipper. Coming from a battleship, he probably would have been comfortable with a spit-and-polish ship. But, he was quick to realize that these young crewmen, trying to master this ungainly ship, had no time or inclination to polish belt buckles. The crew respected him for the confidence and competence he showed in handling his ship in storms, on beaches, in strange harbors, all without a mishap. It was hard to believe that up to the minute he took command in Norfolk, he had never set foot on an LST.

Looking at the log I see that we held captain's mast from time to time. That's a form of drumhead justice visited on crewmen for minor infractions. Captain's mast was what a chief had in mind when he told an erring sailor: "If you don't shape up, I'll have you up before the old man." The procedure was to bring the guilty party (he was always guilty) up to the captain's office where the charges were made. It was usually a charge of absent over leave (AOL). There was never a defense. If the OOD said you were late, you were late. The captain might listen to excuses but few of them ever flew. Punishment was usually in the form of withheld shore leave, no small thing.

Put 100 young men in a crowded space for any length of time and you're going to have a few fights. One of the worst was a bare knuckle scrap between two signalmen in my division, both petty officers. For a while I thought one of them had permanent facial scars. I had the battlers brought up to the flag deck where I gave them an animated lecture intended to be seen by everybody on the open decks. Actually my text wasn't all that strong. I told them we couldn't run a ship with petty officers in open combat and that I would take stern measures if I heard of a repeat performance. Joe LePage of LST 376 (remember Joe's telling of the bombing of LST 158 at Sicily) told me that he came to blows with two of his best buddies.

> *I got into two fights in the tank deck, and both of them were with my best friends in the black gang. I'm sure they were caused by the tension we were going through.*

Neither fight lasted more than a minute or two.

Transition from civilian to Navy officer was an abrupt move. On the day Pearl Harbor was bombed, the Navy knew they were going to need more than 100,000 officers. They didn't exist, so they had to be created. Where to find the raw material? The best source was the regular Navy's own chiefs and warrant officers but there were damned few of them. Besides, if all the chiefs were wearing Lieut (jg) stripes, who was going to run the ships? There was the time limitation. It took four years of intensive study and training at Annapolis to turn out a lowly ensign, but the shipyards were putting out new ships every day. The Navy's solution was to sign up recent college grads and push them through 90 days' training, not on ships but at college campuses. The regular Navy and the enlisted men called these newly minted officers 90-Day Wonders. Lee Hofer of LST 456 tells me that the South Pacific LSTers called them Shirley Temples. Did the Navy do the right thing? Actually they didn't have much choice. How did the program work out? Well, it filled each position with a warm body, and surprisingly many of the Wonders became top-notch officers in a short time. Most of them served reasonably well and others should have stayed home. The worst were those who became obsessed with the authority suddenly thrust upon them. The enlisted men were quick to spot those guys and make life uncomfortable for them.

I had to learn the routine step by step. In my two-and-a-half years on LST 400 I ran four departments: Communications, Ship's Control, Deck and Gunnery. All this stuff was new to me and I didn't get the job done by flashing my gold stripes. The first thing to learn was that petty officers took pride in their jobs. They expected to be told what had to be done but they resented being told how to do it. I learned that while we were still in U.S. waters. I was relieving a night watch and the retiring OOD told me that he was towing a navigational aid, a small wooden platform with a scoop on the bottom leading to a spout on the top. The platform, call it a sea sled, was towed about 500 feet astern where it threw a jet of white water about six feet high. This was to tell the following ship that he was getting too close to your stern. My orders were to haul it in at dawn. About 5:15 AM I told the bosun-of-the-watch to take in the sea sled. He asked me to put another auxiliary generator on line to power the stern winch. "You don't need a winch for that," I told him. "Have a couple of seamen haul it in by hand." He knew that that was impossible and at a later time, when we knew each other better, he would have told me so. But at this point he decided that the young one-striper needed a lesson. He gave me a brisk "aye aye, sir" which I should have caught as being a little too formal, and he disappeared down the ladder. About ten minutes later I wandered aft on the flag bridge to see how the recovery of the sea sled was coming on. I looked down to see the bosun, arms folded, watching four seamen struggling with the hawser and not budging it an inch. I couldn't hear their mutterings or see their expressions, but I got the point. Back at the conning tower I called the engine room to put Auxiliary Generator #3 on the line. I called the bosun to the bridge. "Auxiliary #3 is on line." He acknowledged and soon had the sea sled aboard. End

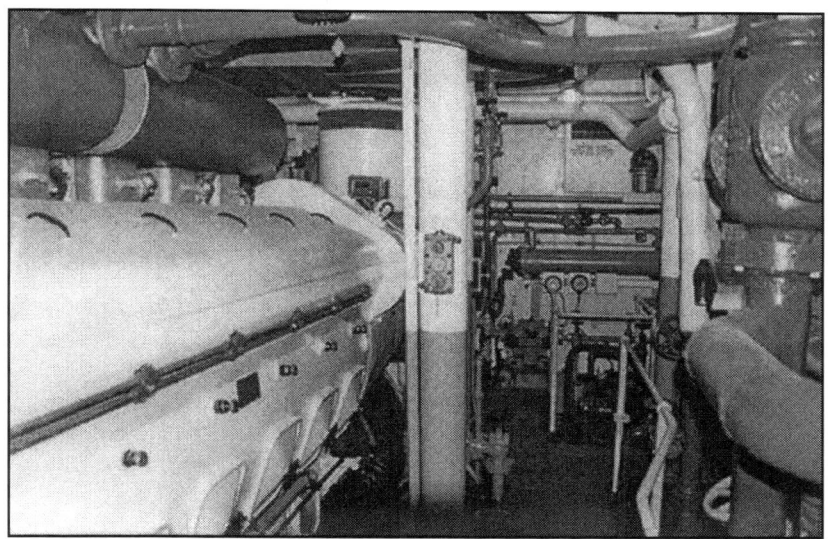

LST Engine Room: 1,200 HP, GM Diesel Main Engine (left) (U.S. Government, public domain)

of episode? Not quite. A few weeks later the bosun wanted an extension on a weekend pass. I saw to it that he got it. We lived happily ever after.

Looking over these pages I see that I have made the crew seem to be made up entirely of raw recruits and a couple of Navy regular chiefs. Not quite true. I have in mind two enlistees who came aboard straight out of civilian life but were highly qualified before the Navy ever saw them. One was a young man from southern Indiana named Grabbe who seemed to have invented diesel engines. He mastered the two 1,200 HP main engines, three auxiliary generators and the diesel-driven LCVPs. You could always tell if one of the engines was in trouble when the loudspeaker called out: "Now hear this, Grabbe, report to the auxiliary engine room, on the double."

The other genius was John Lieber, an old man by our standards. John was a 32-year-old from Pittsburgh who had ten years' experience as a commercial electrician. I can't recall an electrical problem he couldn't handle. Most LSTs had disabling breakdowns in the early stages of operation. With the skipper's ship handling, the savvy of the chiefs and the skill of a few crewmen, LST 400 was kept in good running condition and never missed an assignment throughout the war.

When you draw a crew of 100 men from a pool as large as the United States of America, you're going to a get a mixed bag, including a few really off-beat characters. Joe LePage, the guy who's always at the scene, tells of a guy to remember on his LST:

> *Chief Jones had spent 2 years in China in the Navy and definitely had the Asiatic stare. In the time he spent aboard our ship, anytime you got close to him you could smell liquor. We all wondered where he could stock enough wine or liquor that he could keep supplied. After getting back to the States we found out. The five-gallon wooden kegs that were kept in the small boats (LCVPs) were all loaded with his wine and liquor. He also had an oversupply of gas and he had no qualms about letting it go. His response to anyone who was unlucky enough to be around him was "Did you see that mouse run by?"*

Wartime life aboard an LST cannot be described in a paragraph or, perhaps, even in a book. The confinement, the rolling motion, the lack of amenities and the anxious moments were partly offset by camaraderie, absorbing work, and occasionally watching a sunrise on a peaceful sea. In balancing likes and dislikes, seafaring was like civilian life, only more so.

Descriptions of military life seldom mention the absence of women. I don't mean girlfriends. There's plenty of prose, poetry and drama on that subject. I mean the absence of grandmothers, aunts, family friends and the stranger who smiled when you held a door open for her. This part of our provenance was missing and we all felt it. Our commitment required that we spend a whole year without hearing a little girl giggle. We probably weren't aware that we missed things like that, but we did.

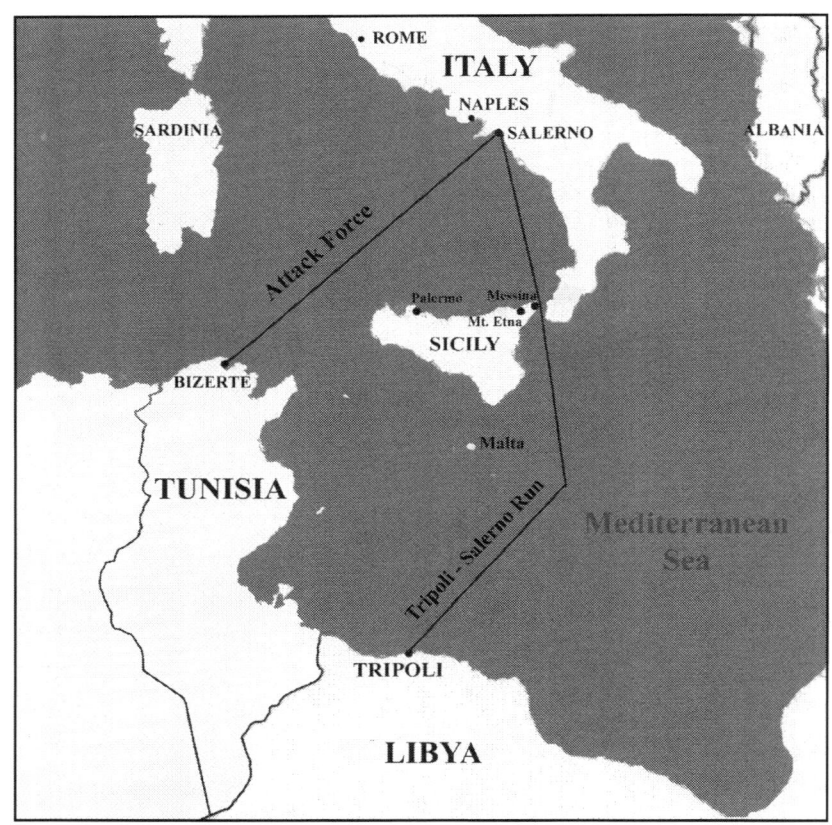

U.S. Attack Force: Bizerte to Salerno

CHAPTER 5

Italy

In October and November of 1943, the Allies were advancing on all fronts. The Red Army forced the Germans out of Russia, retaking Kiev. The U. S. Navy began to retake Japanese-occupied islands with Marine attacks on Tarawa in the Marshalls and Bougainville in the Solomons.

Italy was our next target and we wasted no time getting at it. Axis troops were driven out of Sicily on August 17 and on September 8, LST 400 was combat-loaded and steaming north of Sicily on a northeasterly course. Our destination was the Gulf of Salerno, about 30 miles southeast of Naples. At midmorning the commodore announced the surrender of all Italian forces. That promised to lighten the resistance. We were also told that preliminary bombardment was withheld to maintain an element of surprise. That should have helped, too. Nothing helped. The Germans were waiting at the Salerno beachhead in force. High-level bombing attacks began as soon as we reached the staging area at 2 PM on September 9. Throughout the rest of the day and night we were called to battle stations several times. No bombs fell near us, just the aggravating flares. The invasion fleet continued sporadic anti-aircraft fire throughout the night.

On September 10, we were ordered to land on Green Beach. This landing went according to the books. The Salerno beach was steep enough for us to run our bow up to the shoreline and lay our ramp on the dry sand. In an hour-and-a-half we

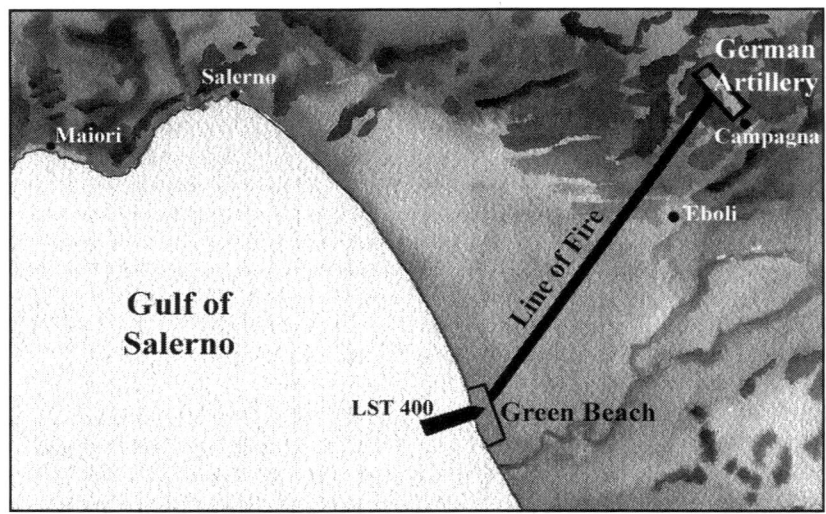

Salerno Beach, September 15, 1943

German 88 mm Gun *(from Bundesarchiv, Wikimedia Commons, 3.0)*

debarked all army vehicles and personnel. This was a very effective Army–Navy joint operation. The GIs wanted to get off the ship; we wanted to get off the beach. When the last truck rolled down the ramp we were hauling in on our stern anchor cable.

The Luftwaffe continued to bomb the staging area with some success. Shortly after we anchored, LST 351 pulled alongside to transfer 32 casualties from the USS *Nauset*, a seagoing tug that had been sunk by German bombers. The *Nauset* had been carrying high-octane gasoline and the survivors were badly burned and disfigured. Their heads appeared to be swollen twice normal size. We did our best to take care of the injured with our limited facilities. Several crewmen pitched in to help the injured on our way back to Bizerte. Bob Brown, ship's cook and later historian, wrote:

> *Remember, we had to feed them through tubes, they were burned so bad. I believe Fred Campbell (chief pharmacist) received an advancement in rating or a commendation for the way he handled those survivors.*

USS **Nauset** *(National Archives: 19-N-42608)*

I heard later that all casualties survived.

We were reloaded and back to the beaches in a day. This time we carried a load of tanks and 254 soldiers. At 3 PM on September 15, we were ordered into Green Beach, the same beach we had hit on our first trip. The beach was still under fire from land guns. The Army/Navy brass on the flagship had a tough call to make. On one hand, if we stayed on the beach in artillery range, one well–placed shot could put our 18 tanks out of action; on the other, they needed the tanks ashore to take out the artillery that was pounding the beach. We pulled into the beach at 2 PM and had just begun to unload when we were ordered back to the staging area. An Army officer standing beside me on the bridge blew his top. He accused the "goddam" Navy of chickening out under fire. I tried to calm him with the pitch that the Army was probably calling for more time to silence the enemy guns before they risked their tanks on the treacherous beach. He didn't buy it. The same old story: the Army wanted to get off the ship.

We beached again at 6:30 PM and as soon as our ramp touched the sand we were ordered to retract. We drew off and had only traveled a thousand yards when we were ordered back to the beach, this time to stay. We did it right again. We got the remaining load off in an hour. But what an hour! The Germans had been watching the whole performance and as soon as our first tank rolled down the ramp, the first shell flew overhead. It passed about twenty feet overhead and detonated about 50 feet to starboard. The next one fell short, about 30 feet off our port beam. We were bracketed, a classic gunnery problem. The gunner's next step was to set his elevation sight midway between his long shot and his short one. I'm sure he tried it and tried it again and again. In all, seventeen rounds were fired at us and not one touched the ship. Under fire, the crew stood to their guns, unloaded tanks and manned the bridge, all exposed positions.

The black gang in the engine room had it even worse, in my mind. They could hear the commotion, but they could see nothing from their compartments deep in the bowels of the ship.

War can be bizarre even in its most terrifying moments. Between rounds, I looked down from the signal bridge on a small, brown-skinned man leaning over the port rail. He was Chief Azuelo, a 40-year-old officer's steward with service stripes from his elbow to his wrist. Another whim of the Bureau of Personnel. The chief belonged in the wardroom of a battleship, not in the galley of an LST. He had taken a break from his galley duties and had stepped out on deck to admire the Sorrento Peninsula like a tourist on a cruise ship. Even as I looked at him a shell hit the water 20 feet in front of him. The shell didn't explode, but it did splash water on the little man. This amused him and seeing me standing on the deck above him he flashed a broad smile and walked back into the galley. I went back up to the conning tower feeling that nothing could happen to this ship.

Chief Officer's Steward, Primitivo Azuelo (courtesy of the author)

Shortly after beaching we put both our landing boats in the water. Each was equipped with a smoke generator that put out a cloud of white fog but not enough to cover the ships. We were still exposed and the shelling continued. A Canadian Corvette saw our plight and came racing across our stern belching a heavy cloud of smoke. This did the trick. Soon I couldn't see our bow, and I hoped the enemy couldn't see it either. They dropped in a few more rounds that we could hear but not see and soon the last Army vehicle rolled down the ramp. Commands poured from the bridge: "Up ramp, close bow doors, haul round on the stern anchor, all engines back one-third." Our bow swung slowly seaward and we felt our way through the smokescreen, heading for the anchorage. We spent a relatively quiet night watching magnesium flares, but none of the bombs fell near us. If the shore guns couldn't hit us, the bombers didn't have a chance.

Our ordeal on the beach wasn't entirely without casualty. Here are a few excerpts from our administrative log:

> *T/5 John Henry remained aboard at the request of the Army commanding officer to be transferred to Army Hospital for hernia operation.*
>
> *Pvt George Anderson at sound of shell overhead fell, or was pushed to the deck causing fracture of right patella.*
>
> *Pvt John Doe was affected with war neurosis during the heavy shelling of the ship while unloading.*
>
> *This man remained on ship without authority. It was not discovered that he was on board until the ship had retracted from the beach.*
>
> *Pvt Edward Smith—same as above.*

At. 7:00 AM the next morning we steamed out of the Gulf of Salerno but this time we were not headed for Bizerte. Our course was southeasterly and at 1:00 AM on September 17, our convoy formed into a single column to pass between Scylla and Charybdis, with Mt. Etna's glow coming up on our starboard bow. Our destination was Tripoli and we didn't know why. The city and port had been heavily involved in the Montgomery–Rommel desert war and it wasn't likely to hold large stores of arms and ammunition for us to haul. But Tripoli was a welcome liberty town, pointing up one of the vagaries of amphibious warfare. One day you could be hammered by shells and bombs, and two days later be wandering tree-lined streets and sampling the wines of a famous Mediterranean seaport. Our Tripoli visit wasn't entirely without conflict. An East–West incident was reported to me by Howard McNamara, a fellow watch officer:

View of Tripoli, Libya (from Wikimedia Commons, public domain)

We all have our favorite war stories and naturally I have one. If you recall, we had a soft spoken boatswain's mate from Virginia named Albin A. George. One day several of us—you may have been one—were on liberty in Tripoli, Libya. We ran into a commotion outside a mosque. "A.A." was the center of the trouble. It seems he had blundered as a non-Moslem into a forbidden area, and a guard was prodding at him with a bayonet. He may very well have executed him on the spot if we hadn't arrived. Somehow, without knowing a word of Arabic, we got it across to the guard that he meant no harm and that we would be responsible for him. We suggested to A.A. that he return to the ship and save his sightseeing for Norfolk.

After two days in port, our Tripoli mission was made clear. We weren't sent there to load tanks; our cargo was to be part of a regiment of British colonial soldiers; I believe they were Sikhs. We took several hundred troops aboard and headed back for the beachhead. I had the midwatch (midnight to 4 AM) somewhere off the southeast corner of Sicily. Late in the watch, First Class Signalman Al Lange reported a torpedo track coming in on the starboard beam. The situation called for hard right rudder which would take ten seconds before the bow began to swing. In that time we would have been hit or missed. Ten seconds passed without a sound. I had my doubts so I questioned Lange. Al and I had spent many hours together on the bridge and our relationship was less formal than you would find on the bridge of a battleship. Our exchange went like this:

Jaeger: "Are you sure you saw a torpedo wake?"

Lange: "You're damn right I saw it."

Jaeger: "I didn't see it."

Lange: "That don't mean nothing."

Those signalmen resented challenges to their visual acuity.

We landed the Sikhs on Salerno beach without incident. The beach was quiet and I yielded to a long standing urge to visit Italy. I wandered north along the shoreline until I saw three soldiers emerge from a thicket and move slowly toward me in a semi-crouch. They wore old WWI helmets so they were either Aussies or Brits. Then I saw why they were crouching. Each was gently probing the sand with the tip of a bayonet. Sappers! My passion for sightseeing was suddenly gratified. Not a word passed between me and the soldiers. They concentrated on their mine-seeking and I retraced my steps literally, each retreating step falling precisely into my advancing footprint in the sand. My tour of Italy would have to wait.

We left Salerno in a convoy on October 10. We were assigned to Flotilla Two which included our colleague LST 325. We moved to Bizerte, then to Oran. Our Mediterranean job was finished.

Back in the relative calm of Algeria, the LST 400 ship's company was ready for rest and recreation. You don't find much rest in a chaotic liberty port like Oran and the recreation is limited to crowded bars and brothels. Both had their risks. I had dry heaves for two days after tangling with bad booze in an Oran barroom. With that episode in mind, I was interested when an ensign I knew from another ship told me where I could get some real, honest-to-god French cognac. The labels and seals looked authentic so I bought four bottles for future reference. Since alcoholic beverages were banned from Navy ships, I had a logistics problem. Being an old LST hand at this time, I was adept at handling strange cargo. I knew that our mail clerk was ashore and that he would soon be returning from the fleet post office with a canvas bag of the ship's mail. The clerk, as you will recall, was a happy-go-lucky kid from upstate Vermont. I knew he wouldn't object to a little smuggling so I caught up with him on his way back to the ship and stashed the four bottles in the mail bag. I went back to the open market and he went back to the ship. I sent for him next morning and he showed up at my cabin—empty handed. How come? Well, it was a long story involving a procedure called "nesting." A crowded harbor like Oran could accommodate all ships only if they moored several ships at one docking space. The first ship tied to the dock. The second ship tied outboard of the first ship, the third tied outboard the second—"nesting." Each ship had the OOD posted at the rail and in Navy tradition when you wanted to set foot aboard a ship, you saluted the OOD and asked his permission to come aboard. LST 400 was nested outboard and the mail clerk had to cross two ships to get to us. At the second gangway he was feeling the strain and decided to shift the mail sack from one shoulder to the other. You could hear the bottles clanking all over the harbor. The OOD took the mail clerk aside, relieved him of the contraband and sent him on his way. I immediately crossed over to his ship to make sure he didn't report the mail clerk. He promised he wouldn't do that but, he was sorry to say, he couldn't allow further passage of the guilty bottles over a U.S. Navy ship. I got the message and could only console myself with the thought that I was to host a party for a group of fellow LST sailors at some future date. I was lucky at that. If the OOD had been a by-the-book guy, I could have been charged not only with smuggling alcohol aboard ship but also with corrupting the mail clerk—both court martial offenses.

Rock of Gibraltar with Search Lights (United Kingdom Government, public domain)

On November 8 we moored to Quay du Senegal in Oran harbor while a huge crane slowly lowered another LCT on our main deck. Back in March this same ritual foretold a long sea voyage. It was the same story here. On November 22, our flotilla was steaming single file out of Oran harbor to join Convoy MKS 31, headed for Gibraltar and out into the Atlantic Ocean.

As far as I know, passing through the Straits of Gibraltar calls for no ceremony like that of crossing the equator. On this occasion, however, LST 400 held a private ritual that will not become established in maritime lore. Watch Officer Howard McNamara was not a hard man to please. Cramped shipboard life, rolling sea, long watches—these he took in stride, but he could not abide onions. Unfortunately he had mentioned this at the wardroom table as we were passing the Rock on our way into the Mediterranean the previous May. Like the rest of us, Mac looked forward to the time when, having completed our dirty business in the Med, we would pass the Rock on our way out of the Med on our way home. In fact, he carelessly remarked that he'd be so glad to see the Rock on our starboard side that he'd eat a raw onion. That bit of hyperbole, intended only to brighten the conversation, was immediately forgotten by all, with one exception: the skipper.

Somewhat out of character, the captain pressed the matter. Mac claimed that while we were passing the Rock to starboard alright, we weren't going home. We were headed to England to join in on the invasion of the European mainland. But, as Lawyer Chatterton pointed out, Mac's statement in front of witnesses constituted a verbal contract. He then polled the rest of us to see if anybody recalled a codicil releasing the contractor if our destination was any place other that the U.S. Mac got no help from his shipmates. Five months of war had drained us of human compassion. McNamara can still taste onions when the wind is in the east.

Five months had passed since we entered the Mediterranean. Our young sailors were only five months older but their ship now had a veteran crew. They had not only learned to handle the new ship, they were now able to do it under fire. No one overcomes the revulsion felt when someone fires a lethal weapon at him but these youngsters had learned to deal with fear. They stuck to their guns in spite of the incoming hardware. That's courage.

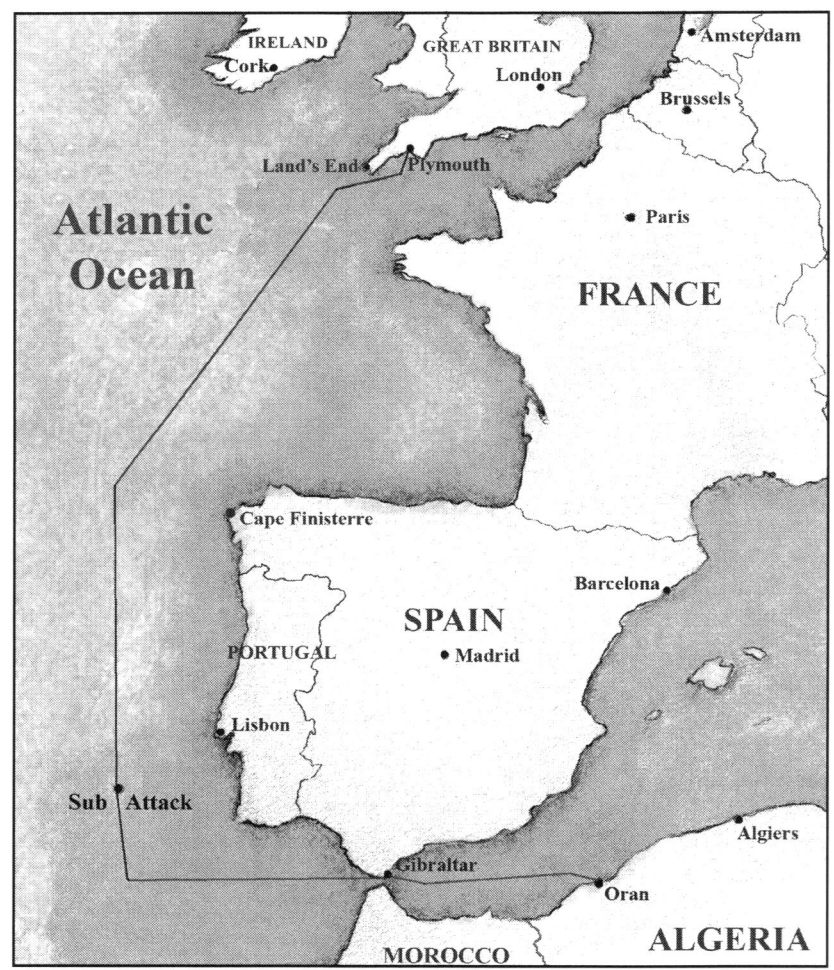

North Africa to England

Chapter 6

United Kingdom

The Allied Forces battled their way up the Italian peninsula throughout the winter of 1943–1944. The ill-fated landings at Anzio were made on January 22, 1944, and Monte Cassino was attacked in March. The U.S. Navy continued to press across the central Pacific, taking the Marshall Islands on February 2, 1944.

We left Gibraltar behind us in the last week of November, 1943. One of the quartermasters pointed out that if we stayed on our present course we'd be in Norfolk in two weeks. But SHAEF (Supreme Headquarters Allied Expeditionary Forces) had other plans. Stalin's pressure for a second front had the support of no less than General George C. Marshall. Both wanted the Allies to forget the Mediterranean and attack across the English Channel in 1943. Churchill was opposed and his view prevailed.

Now, with our troops firmly established in Italy and North Africa, there was no reason to delay the Channel crossing. On November 25 we made the fateful right turn and headed north up the coast of Portugal. About that time I noticed white smoke arising from several ships at the front of the convoy. The skipper pointed out that the smoke was white, not the dreaded black, oily stuff. As he spoke, a signalman handed him a message from the commodore ordering us to commence a smoke generator drill. Not a bad idea in light of our experience at Salerno.

At noon the next day we called the crew to battle stations for the first time since leaving Gibraltar. The screening destroyers were dropping depth charges about two miles off our port bow. There wasn't much we could do but keep station and watch with great interest. The battle lasted a half hour and we speculated that the destroyers may have reacted to a false echo. We went to battle stations again the next day, pointing our guns, but not firing them, at a lone Fw200.

There was no doubt about the next incident. At 2:30 AM on November 28 we sounded General Quarters, the howling alarm that calls crews to their battle stations. It is a loud, rasping, pulsating sound that brings you from the deepest coma to round-eyed alert on the first blast. The loudspeakers were placed about the ship in such a way that it seemed as if you were never more than 18 inches away from one. By the time you got to your battle station you forgot that there ever was such a thing as sleep. This time the escorts really had a fight on their hands. All we could do was try to keep station in total darkness. LST 345 was a few ships ahead in our column. Here's an entry from their captain's November 28, 1943, War Diary:

> *0000 Steaming as before. Speed 9 knots. 0035 Occasional flares ahead of convoy. 0243 All hands to General Quarters. More flares and flashes. Later was informed by flag hoist from SOPA that one U-Boat had been sunk definitely and nine driven off by escorting British corvettes.*

Shortly before dawn I saw gunfire two miles astern. I learned that one of the subs, damaged in the battle, had surfaced to slug it out with our escort. At sunrise I noticed that the two Canadian corvettes covering our rear had vanished. They were the ones who had taken on the surfaced submarines. When they returned to their position in the screen at breakfast time, I recalled that it was a Canadian corvette that had saved our bacon at Salerno. If I ever find that I need a bodyguard, he'll sure as hell be Canadian.

We were heading to a point off Cape Finisterre on the northwest corner of Spain. The name Finisterre (land's end) caught

Canadian Corvette (from Bryson 109, public domain)

my eye because my dead reckoning course line lead to a promontory at the southwest corner of England, also known as Land's End. Our run from the Spanish "Land's End" to the English "Land's End" was not to be forgotten. Whenever I'm with LST veterans the conversation soon turns to storms at sea. With Pacific vets it's usually the typhoon off Okinawa that capsized

Ship in Storm (U.S. Government, public domain)

three destroyers. With European vets it's one of several North Atlantic gales. They were all vicious. Ours started somewhere southwest of Cape Finisterre and lasted until we entered the English Channel. That 1,000 mile run should have taken us four and a half days; it took eight. Unlike the storm that hit us at Sicily, this one started slowly but at the end of the first night it was a full force gale. The convoy was heading just east of true north and the wind came from just west of north—right on the port bow again.

The wind came on at 70-plus miles per hour and held steady for a week. Station keeping was difficult. When we slid down into the trough of a huge wave, the helmsman would lose sight of the ship ahead in column in spite of the fact that his masthead was 70 feet above sea level. (Was there ever such a thing as a level sea?) Old seamen prided themselves on being able to walk the deck unsupported in a rolling sea but with the ship rolling thirty degrees from side to side even the saltiest sailor grabbed onto anything that helped him stay erect. Standing watch in the conning tower, though tiring, was possible with the aid of the shoulder-high combing surrounding it. It was the storm's interference with life's basic functions that wore us down. Eating became a chore. We laid wet towels on the table to keep our plates from sliding off. Not good enough. We still had to hold the plate with one hand and the fork with the other. Even that didn't stop the salt and pepper shakers from flying into our laps. Several of us gave up table dining and ate our cheese and baloney sandwiches standing up.

Sleeping, if it could be done at all, was made possible by wedging yourself into the bunk with pillows or some other bulk material. A sort of twilight sleep could be managed by lying face down and grasping the bunk bottom. Washing and showering were difficult. Other lavatory services I leave to your imagination.

LST designers had to make tough choices. Their primary job was to design a ship that could land tanks on an ocean beach. That called for a flat bottom and a shallow draft. But before they

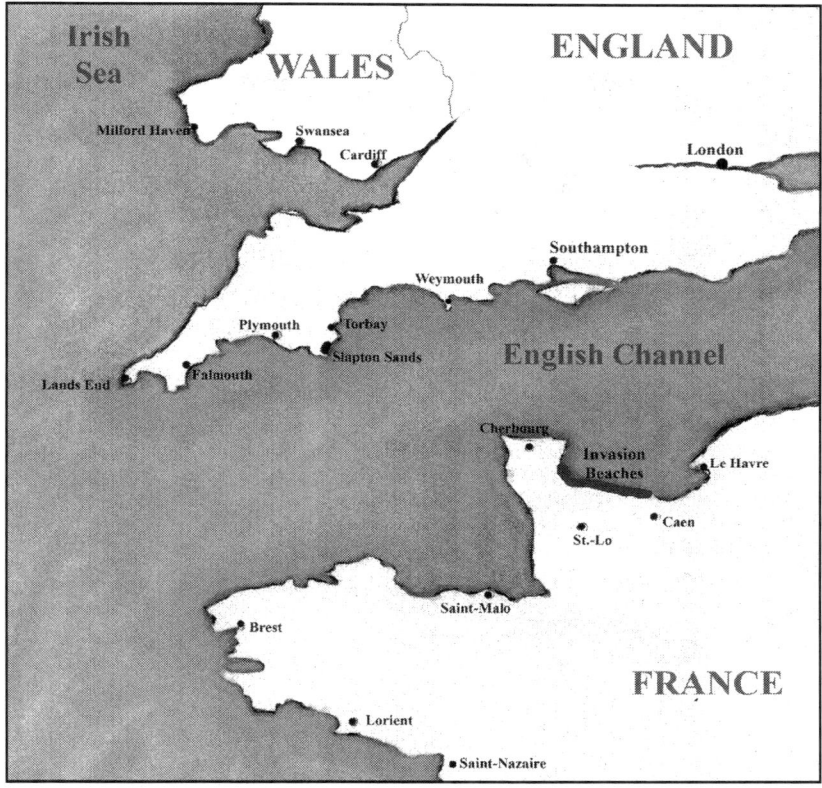

English Channel

could land the tanks they had to get them there. That called for a seaworthy ship. The beaching factor prevailed. In a high sea the ships would have to do the best they could. Driving an LST into a heading sea was almost intolerable. The shallow draft kept the hull near the water's surface, making sure that it got all the action the waves had to offer. The blunt bow made sure that the ship rode on top of the waves, not through them like ships with the traditional sharp stem. LSTs had another vulnerability: they were built with a light framework and a thin skin, causing the main deck to ripple when the bow crashed into an oncoming wave. Our main deck actually split open during a storm on the English Channel. When I boarded LST 325 in Peoria in 2007, I checked its main deck. Sure enough, steel plates were welded in a line extending from rail to rail directly forward of the deckhouse. The wartime first-aid laid down 63 years earlier was still in place.

We were nearing exhaustion on December 5 when we passed the Isle of Scilly and headed up the English Channel. By mid-afternoon we sighted Eddystone Light. For centuries that famous lighthouse has been telling sea-weary sailors to take heart—safe harbor is only fifteen miles away. At 7:00 PM we were tied to a mooring buoy in Plymouth Harbor enjoying simple things like eating sitting down, a hot shower and a good night's sleep, and, if you were lucky, mail from home.

The commodore had no immediate plans for us so we enjoyed a week of easy living, doing routine chores and enjoying a few hours ashore in wartime Plymouth. We couldn't be completely at ease with the cumbersome LCT still on our back, so we were pleased to get orders sending us up the Channel to Portsmouth where a heavy floating crane relieved us of that burden. Nine-hundred tons lighter, we turned back down the Channel past Plymouth to Falmouth where we celebrated Christmas in dry dock. A shipmate got hold of a jeep and we drove out to Land's End. We had seen this sea cliff from the ocean a few weeks back. The view was equally striking from

Eddystone Light *(from Wikimedia Commons, public domain)*

the land. Looking down we could see waves driven all the way from Bermuda crashing against this historic rock. In our drive around, I insisted on having a look at places with romantic names like St. Ives and Penzance. I expected to see Stonehenge thereabouts, but my better-informed companion told me that the ancient landmark lay better than halfway to London.

A sightseeing tour of southwest England would have suited me fine but the flotilla commander felt that we needed more beaching practice. On the first day of 1944 a convoy of trucks rolled into Falmouth with the GIs who were to share our drill. On January 2, with 293 soldiers aboard, we left Falmouth for a night run up the English Channel to a practice beach near Dartmouth, at the southeast corner of Devon. The practice beach is called Slapton Sands, a new name to us then. In a few months it was to become a name we would never forget. We started our mock invasion the next day and to all appearances it was going well when we rounded Start Point and headed for the staging area. Landing craft moved on and off the beach, planes made low-level runs and ships lying well offshore were firing live ammunition at selected targets. I read that our troops suffered "friendly fire" casualties, the first of several command foul-ups. The flotilla commander made our landing realistic by ordering us to the beach and then recalling us three times before we actually landed. Shades of Salerno. Our unloading of trucks and personnel went well, but just before we pulled off the beach an Army captain came up to the conning tower to tell us that one of his trucks was stalled on our tank deck. He asked us to take it with us to Plymouth where he'd pick it up in a few days. Further, he wanted to know if he could leave a couple of GIs aboard to watch the truck. We expected to reload in Plymouth shortly, so we were glad to accommodate our Army colleague. We anchored in Plymouth the next afternoon waiting for an order to approach the dock for reloading. That order never came. Instead, we were ordered to head for Wales, empty. Empty, that is, except for an Army truck, a sergeant and a corporal.

Left: H.C. Kay, Titusville, NJ. Right: E.N. Isaksen, Brooklyn, NY. These two men were experts at using the 36' LCVPs as harbor tugs. (both photos courtesy of the author)

Seagoing ships move slowly in harbors; so slowly that they do not respond to their rudders. That is why harbor pilots require tugboats to push and pull ships into position. Tugboats, as well as harbor pilots, were seldom available in the war zone. LST skippers learned to use their versatile LCVPs as tugboats. With heavy rope matting draped over the bow and manila lines extending from the bow and stern, the boats were able to push or pull on the ship's bow or stern as needed. Captain Lyden became expert at using the LCVPs and Coxswains Kay and Isaksen became equally proficient at maneuvering the boats on shouted orders from the ship. We kept one of the LCVPs alongside at all times when moving in the harbor, picking it up on-the-run as we left. At 9:45 AM on January 12, 1944, we pulled away from our mooring and headed out of Plymouth harbor. Passing the sea buoy, we called the LCVP alongside and shackled it to the steel cables leading down from the davits (hoists). With the crew still aboard, we started hauling the boat up to the boat deck. It had just cleared the water when the forward starboard davit collapsed and fell into the boat. The three-ton steel davit could kill anyone it fell on. I rushed to the starboard bridge wing to look down on two crewmen lying in the bottom of the boat—unhurt. Cox'n Reggie Atkinson saw the davit coming down and leaped over the stern and was now swimming for his life as the ship pulled away. I called for a life line and buoy but the aft line handlers were way ahead of me. We lowered the port boat to pick Reggie up and soon we had all three aboard without a scratch. In peacetime that incident would have called for a full Board of Inquiry. We briefly described the incident in the log and got on with the war.

With a healthy crew aboard we passed Eddystone Light outbound. This time we moved down Channel and rounded Land's End heading north to Milford Haven, a sheltered bay at the southwest tip of Wales. This place was well named. I don't know what "Milford" signifies, but there's no question about the place being a haven. The bay opens on Bristol Channel at its west end and extends east for ten miles through farmland and small villages. We moved east and moored to a buoy off the town of Milford Haven. We stayed there for a month. The Haven was home for much of the British fishing fleet, many of whose

LCVP Being Hoisted Aboard an LST (National Archives: SC 181041)

larger vessels were now rigged with anti-submarine gear and were busy escorting Allied ships through home waters. Smaller and older vessels were still fishing, doing their best to feed their beleaguered country. One of the oldest and smallest was pressed into service as a water taxi taking sailors to and from Milford Haven and Pembroke. A big night in the Haven was a water taxi trip to a pub in Pembroke for a pint or two of bitters (British beer). As in Bermuda, the war was remote.

About this time there was a change in our deck duties. U. S. armed forces were still expanding rapidly and the peacetime practice of promoting officers on merit alone had to be dropped in favor of mass advancement based on length of service only. It worked like this: when the Navy commissioned an officer, he was given a serial number, say 171536. The next guy through the door would be given number 171537, and so on. When the expanding fleet needed higher rankings, the Bureau of Personnel would send a radio signal (ALNAV) saying that every ensign having a serial number between 143746 and 188603 was hereby promoted one rank. In the winter of 1944 I became a lieutenant, junior grade. That wasn't the only change. Executive Officer Jim Campbell was transferred and Gunnery Officer Joe Gettys took his place. I took Joe's place. The change from communications to gunnery wasn't as drastic as it sounds. I'd had no experience with guns but at the time I felt that, with a good chief, I could command the Pacific fleet. Our battery of anti-aircraft guns wasn't imposing enough to rate a chief, but we did have a reliable second class gunner's mate. The guns were kept in top shape with little oversight on my part. I kept busy with my jobs navigating and standing deck watches.

We enjoyed the seclusion of Milford Haven in company with our new army guests. The truck on the tank deck was no burden and the two soldiers adapted well to Navy life. They had become friendly with the crew and pitched in voluntarily on work details. The only thing that marked them apart was their brown khaki garb and that became a problem. One-third of the crew was allowed ashore every night and the soldiers were free to

Gunnery Division, May 1944: *Top row: G. Scalamoni, D. Bingham, W. Lederle, J. Burba; bottom row: unknown, C. Epperson, Lt (jg) Gene Jaeger, H.E. Lowdermilk, P. Terefenko. (courtesy of the author)*

accompany them. They told the chief bosun that if they were seen in Army dress in this remote naval outpost they were likely to be picked up as AWOL or worse. They were sure they could eventually prove their status but they were afraid that they might face some brig time before they did so. The chief suggested that they dress in navy blue and go ashore with their new shipmates. Sounded OK to me but I thought we ought to let the captain in on the plot. It was alright with the old man, so our soldier/sailors spent a few nights in Milford/Pembroke in Navy uniform.

On February 15 we were ordered to sail up the Bristol Channel to Swansea for more intensive beaching practice. Like most European ports that I saw, Swansea harbor was equipped with paved extensions of city streets that ran to the water's edge and continued out into the water a hundred feet or more. These ramps were called "hards" and they were designed to handle ferry boats. They worked well for the bow-loading LSTs and we were soon called into the hard for a practice load. But first, we had to get rid of the Army truck on our tank deck and, of course, our two khaki-clad crewmen. Apparently they had established their bona fides with local Army authorities. They drove their truck up the hard and vanished into the streets of Swansea. I hope they fared well in the coming storm.

Our decks cleared, we loaded a motorized Army unit and hauled it an hour's run to Oxwich or Port Eynon where we beached, unloaded, retracted and then headed back to Swansea to do it all over again. We did this for several days till it became routine and I said as much to one of the Army officers. "Maybe you don't need the practice," he said, "but we do." Actually we needed it too. You can't get too good at beaching. A successful landing called for skill. Hit the beach too hard and you damage your ship or its cargo. Hit it at an angle other than perpendicular and you might broach. There were several LSTs lying broadside to a beach when the war ended. Dropping the stern anchor on the approach called for good timing. Drop it too soon and you were doomed to watch the end of the anchor cable pay off the winch and disappear into the sea. The retraction could be tricky too. There was always the possibility of over-running your anchor cable. A ship with a cable wrapped around its propellers was a ship out of action.

Swansea turned out to be a good liberty town. "Liberty" in Navy parlance is the freedom to go ashore and do what pleased you as long as you returned to the ship by midnight. "Leave" on the other hand, is permission to stay ashore overnight or for several days, a freedom seldom granted us when we were in Europe. Liberties ranged from a hilarious night on the town to nothing more that a pint of ale in a rundown saloon (pub in Britain). Occasionally the best part of the night was the midnight gathering at the dock waiting for boats to take us back to our ships. The levels of intoxication there ranged from dead sober, through boisterous shouting to falling down drunk. One sailor on our flotilla actually did fall into an empty dry dock. I liked the exuberant ones best. A young sailor on the half-lit dock at Swansea stands out in my memory. He was regaling farm life back in Iowa and was particularly proud of a team of mules (not all farms had tractors then). The young Iowan kept repeating in a loud and cheerful voice that "Old Nick and Dick can pull the ass out of any tractor ever built."

It was on February 26, 1944, that we were ordered to Londonderry in Northern Ireland. Why Londonderry? It was beginning to look like our itinerary was being laid out, not by SHAEF, but by the Acme Travel Agency. We anchored in Lough Foyle on the evening of the 29th. Was 1944 a leap year? The stay in Ireland was uneventful. Our tourist routine was limited by the fact that Londonderry lies on the border between Northern Ireland, part of the British Commonwealth, and the Republic of Ireland, an independent state. Northern Ireland was at war with Germany; the Republic of Ireland was not. One step across the border into County Donegal and we were subject to internment as a belligerent. Having both German and Irish grandparents, I was careful to avoid any semblance of belligerence, so I took a peaceful train ride to Belfast. Fraternizing with enlisted men was frowned upon and only one officer could be away overnight, so I traveled alone. The train to Belfast was an antique and the industrial port itself put me in mind of the 19th century's "dark, satanic mills." Probably not a fair assessment of Belfast. What could you expect of an industrial city in a war zone? Two days later I was back on the ship as we pulled out of Lough Foyle and headed east. I took a long look at the west bank so I could tell my Irish-loving father that I had seen County Donegal.

With a couple of invasions behind us our planners decided that our 3", 50 gun served little purpose. It was ineffective against low flying aircraft and when we were beached it was pointed in the wrong direction. The flag deck stood between the gun and the beach. On one of our infrequent practice firings, the gunnery officer tried to see how far forward he could point the piece without telling the bridge crew what he was up to. The muzzle blast nearly took the top of my head off. I still can't hear out of my right ear. The Navy decided to replace the three-incher with a twin 40 mm mount and to add other AA

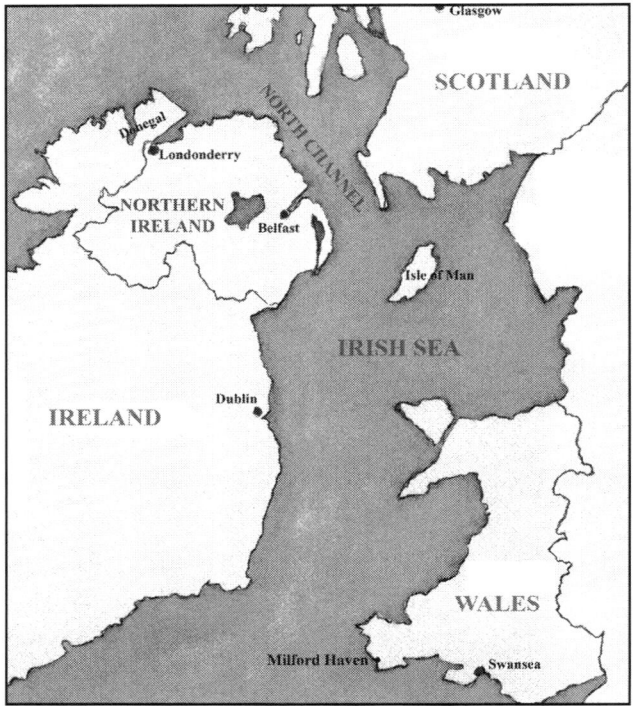

Irish Sea

guns as well. I can't recall if the gun replacement was done in Londonderry or at our next port-of-call, Glasgow. Our stay in Scotland was brief. All I can recall of Glasgow is a shipyard working day and night and a city with a mix of centuries-old buildings and a modern commercial center.

April found us back in Falmouth waiting for another turn at the dry dock. This time we needed paint. After a year of salt spray it was hard to tell if the ship's basic color was gray/blue or rust/brown. Our skipper didn't share the Navy's passion for paint. He had survived the bombing of the USS *California* and he recalled how readily a half-inch coat of paint burst into flame. We were painted and afloat in Falmouth Harbor when orders came to move up the Channel again, this time back to Plymouth.

By this time all thoughts were on the upcoming invasion. A few of us had fallen into the habit of greeting one another with the first line of a popular song. For instance, I might say to a passing shipmate "What is this thing called love" or "Where have all the roses gone," apropos of absolutely nothing. Our Ensign Al Krezdorn told me he used this inanity on a guy at the base. "For all you know we may never meet again," said Al. "What the hell do you mean by that," snapped the clerk. Clearly tension was growing.

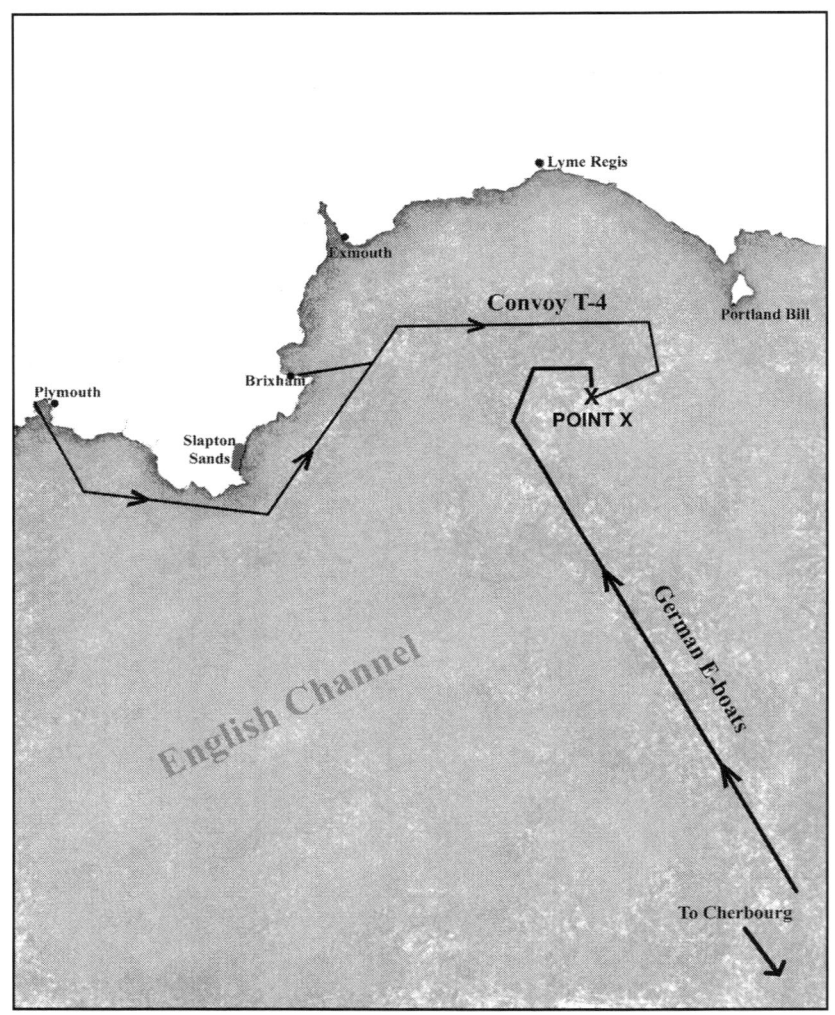

Exercise Tiger

CHAPTER 7

Prelude to Normandy

In the spring of 1944, the Allies made little progress in Italy or on the western front. British and American troops entered Rome on June 5. Soviet troops occupied the Crimea in April and recaptured Sevastopol on May 9. In the Pacific, American troops invaded New Guinea in April and Saipan in June. U.S. carrier planes shot down 220 Japanese planes in the "Mariana Turkey Shoot" on June 15.

Since arriving in England the 400 had cruised on the fringe of the European side of World War II. The waters were troubled with U-Boats and mines, but our group hadn't had a serious loss since we left the beaches of Italy. That was about to end.

The English Channel separated the Allied and Axis armies by about a hundred miles, much less at Dover. In late April of 1944, the British side of the Channel was an arsenal of guns, tanks, planes and the military stores to sustain a million fighting men. The French side, or should I call it the German side, was armed too. But there was a big difference. The Allied command could move their men and equipment freely over England's roads, fly their planes in its skies and move their ships along its coast. The Germans could move on French roads only at the risk of being spotted and destroyed by Allied aircraft. Channel air space was denied German fliers and their airfields were pushed well back into the mainland. Channel waters were denied to all German surface ships with the hard-to-explain exception of a squadron of E-Boats (German torpedo boats) lying untroubled in Cherbourg harbor, a deep-water port on the north coast of France.

Our London headquarters (SHAEF) was so sure of its control of the English Channel that it felt free to conduct pre-invasion landing exercises at Slapton Sands on Lyme Bay only 90 miles from the enemy stronghold at Cherbourg. We had used Slapton Sands for a practice landing the previous January. We didn't know it at the time, but Slapton Sands was chosen for our mock invasion because of its similarity to a beach on the east side of the Cotentin peninsula in Normandy. That beach, shortly to be known to the world as Utah Beach, was similar to Slapton Sands in tidal range, beach gradient and low-lying inshore bluffs. The 3,000 residents of the farms and villages lying adjacent to the Sands had been evacuated. General Joseph L. Collins, VII Corps, had been practicing on this beach since December. The final pre-invasion run on Slapton Sands, Exercise Tiger, was scheduled for the last week of April. Exercise Tiger turned out to be an epic blunder, one for the history books. But history, for the most part, has ignored this grim story.

Our role in Exercise Tiger began at Plymouth. We were called into the hard where we loaded the usual consignment of troops and trucks. We sailed out and past our now-familiar guide, the Eddystone Lighthouse and rounded the southeast tip of County Devon. On the evening of April 26, we anchored off Slapton Sands. The mock invasion was already in progress. Landing craft of all shapes and sizes were leaving south England ports carrying the same cargo they would be carrying when they invaded northern France. Generals Eisenhower, Bradley, Montgomery and Collins were there to watch. LST 400 lay about two miles off the beach, awaiting orders. To our surprise we were ordered to sail out into Lyme Bay and then back to Slapton Sands, to simulate the distance we would run to our still undisclosed target on D-Day. On April 27 we headed northeast along the west coast of Lyme Bay to a point off Exmouth, then east past Lyme Regis, then southeast to a point about fifteen miles off Portland Bill, call it Point X. We were now in a position to make a direct run west to our designated beach on Slapton Sands. This we did, arriving in the early evening. We had no sooner anchored than we were ordered to move in closer to the beach. Finally anchored for the night, the crew and guests fed and bedded, I took a brief nap before heading for the bridge for my night watch. I stopped in the chart room to check for landmarks to watch; dragging anchor was always a threat. I climbed up to the conning tower for a briefing from the OOD I was relieving. All quiet. I relieved the watch.

The next episode occurred just outside my visual range. My description of it here is taken from letters and articles written, much later, by participants. Official military comment at the time was nonexistent…for good reason.

My watch started with a scan of the horizon. Nothing moving, at least nothing that I could see. Men and machines continued to move ashore in total darkness. Some of the invasion fleet was still approaching from the east. Convoy T-4, consisting of eight LSTs loaded largely with U.S. Army personnel, had just passed Point X and was headed toward us. A convoy of that size, operating in hostile waters, would typically be in a tight formation screened fore, aft and on the flanks by escort vessels. T-4, for some reason, was strung out in a long, highly-vulnerable, single file and protected by a single escort. The HMS *Azalea*, an old sub-chaser capable of only 15 knots, was steaming far in front, leaving the convoy exposed on the flanks and in the rear. It has been reported that the Royal Navy headquarters in Plymouth actually ordered two escorts for T-4: the *Azalea* and HMS *Scimitar*, a World War I destroyer. Unfortunately, the *Scimitar* had been damaged in a collision in Plymouth harbor the day before and due to a communication foul-up, headquarters was never informed. As a result eight LSTs , carrying over 1,000 troops, were steaming in the dangerous, darkened English Channel—unprotected.

A night watch at anchor may sound boring, but there were compensations. In the early hours of April 28, 1944, I found myself enjoying the quiet immensity of the darkened sea and sky.

Signalman Lange and I exchanged a few remarks. We had spent many of these nights together and there wasn't much left to say. I sent the messenger below for coffee. While we drank our coffee, T-4 was heading our way at a reduced speed, timed to reach the beaches at sunrise. I scanned the horizon, but couldn't see that another group had moved into pitch black Lyme Bay. A squadron of German E-Boats had left Cherbourg harbor undetected and was now approaching Point X. The squadron was led by S-130, under command of Oberleutnant Gunter Rabe, a highly successful predator known as The Raven. The S-130 (the S is for *Schnellboot*) was 115 feet long, armed with four torpedoes and driven by powerful engines capable of 35 knots. The rest of the Raven's squadron was of similar destructive power. The group, which had been operating in the North Sea out of Rotterdam, had shifted their base to Cherbourg in the past winter, intent on preying on the heavy Allied shipping in the English Channel. In retrospect, it is hard to see why the Allies, with their superior airpower, allowed this to happen. The USAAF and the RAF controlled the skies over Cherbourg. Both air forces were striking targets deep in northern France. Allied warships could steam in sight of the opening of Cherbourg harbor. And yet the E-Boat squadron maintained a base there, unmolested until the VII Corps occupied the city a month after D-Day.

I went below to the chart house, mostly to break the routine, but also to look up the tidal movements for the coming day. We were scheduled, like convoy T-4, to beach at daybreak. The range between high and low tides would tell me how long we would be held on the beach. The quartermaster was catching up on the log. I looked over his shoulder at the most recent entries and returned to the conning tower. A light breeze had sprung up and I could hear the small waves lapping at our waterline.

Out on the Channel, the Raven was searching for targets. He had penetrated Lyme Bay, passed Point X and was well north of T-4's straggling line of LSTs. One account says that at this point the S-Boats received a message from their Cherbourg headquarters, giving them T-4's location and ordering them to attack. Whether by order or by chance, the Raven spotted T-4 sometime after 1:30 AM.

I joined my co-watchers in the conning tower. The ship had swung on the tide and we were now pointing due north. The messenger was staring over the starboard bridge wing, due east. He called up to me. "Did you see that, Mr. Jaeger?" I scanned the eastern horizon followed by a sweep with the binoculars. Nothing. Signalman Lange hadn't seen anything either. The youngster said he thought he saw flashes of light but he wasn't going to argue with a signalman 1/c and the OOD.

The S-Boats had split up in the search for the convoy. Then two of them came upon the absolutely unprotected LSTs at the rear of the long column. The Raven wrote in his log:

> *Shortly before 0200 we saw in the southeast indistinct shadows of a long line of ships that we did not immediately identify as LSTs. At 0207 (after firing two torpedoes) we saw that we had hit the target. Fire was spreading from bow to stern rapidly and a dense cloud of smoke rose from the ship.*

The Raven's squadron had hit LST 507, the last ship in the convoy. Alerted by the flame, the other S-Boats moved in and the whole convoy was targeted. The flames from LST 507 also alerted the *Azalea* to the fact that the convoy it was guarding was under attack. All LST crews rushed to battle stations to bring their anti-aircraft batteries to bear on a surface attack, but the swift S-Boats were hard to find on the partially lit sea. While the survivors of the 507 battled flames, LST 531, in mid-convoy, was torpedoed amidship and sank in seven minutes. The S-Boats continued the attack. Those that had exhausted their supply of torpedoes strafed the LST decks with 20 mm guns. One passed so closely under the bow of an LST that the crew couldn't depress their guns sufficiently to fire on it. The *Azalea* which had turned to face the enemy was unable to fire a single round.

LST 289 was next to last in column. With LST 507 burning just astern, it was able to fire a few rounds but their 20 and 40 mm guns were no match for the S-Boat torpedoes. The 289 was torpedoed in the stern, disabling its main power drive but missing its auxiliary engines. With the assistance of surviving T-4 LSTs it was able to limp ashore.

The casualties were appalling. Men were killed in the torpedo explosions, others jumped over the side only to have their necks broken because they hadn't removed their helmets or died of hypothermia in the cold waters of the English Channel. Others drowned because their inflatable life belts were fastened around their waists rather than under their shoulders. Worst of all were those who were burned alive on the tank deck in flames fed by the fuels from gasoline tanks of onboard vehicles. Bodies washed up on the shores of Lyme Bay for weeks after the disaster. In all, 750 men were lost while we floated calmly on the darkened ocean 45 miles to the west. Soon our relief was heard coming up the ladder. In good time. I was beginning to think seriously about a warm bunk. I briefed the relieving OOD, Lt (jg) McNamara. When he gave me the traditional "I relieve you," I replied, "quiet gig, Mac, good night."

The battle was over. The S-Boats, fearing daylight, headed for harbor. LST 507 was still afloat but sinking slowly, the 289 was being towed to port and the 531 rested on the bottom. Joseph Balkoski had this to say in his excellent book *Utah Beach:*

> *The* Schnelleboote *attack killed about 550 U.S. Army soldiers and 200 U.S. Navy sailors, and injured about 300 more. Two U.S. Army companies, the 3206th Quartermaster Service Company and the 557th Quartermaster Railhead Company, were nearly all annihilated, leaving only a few dazed survivors, men who at one time had considered themselves fortunate to be members of outfits that were not expected to fight in the front line.*
>
> *But on April 28, 1944, Lyme Bay itself was the front line.*

Much has been made of the official cover-up of the Exercise Tiger disaster. Certainly SHAEF slapped the tightest security on the matter, and with good reason. In wartime, the people's right to know also becomes the enemy's right to know. The Germans already knew that they had scored direct hits on some LSTs, but it was all carried out in darkness or in the limited light provided by burning ships. The Germans didn't know the full extent of the damage and SHAEF didn't want to enlighten them. The number of LSTs available for an assault on northern France had become a critical issue and the less the enemy knew about it, the better. It was also pointed out that some of the missing personnel had been cleared for D-Day plans and that there was a chance that some of them had been taken alive. That was a long shot but there was a helluva lot at stake and it must have been a consideration when Ike made his decision to attack Normandy on June 5, only five weeks later. And, very importantly, could the brass let the troops know of such an egregious blunder just before sending them up against Fortress Europa. SHAEF did sit on the casualty list until August when they released it with the invasion casualty list where it was buried with the monumental D-Day story. I'm told that the story was released in the Army newspaper *Stars and Stripes* in July, 1944. I didn't see it although I always made an effort to get a copy of *Stars and Stripes* to see my favorite cartoon characters, not Mauldin's Willie and Joe—I preferred Baker's Sad Sack. I heard the details of Exercise Tiger long after I was separated from the armed services.

Who was to blame? No one individual can be singled out. Twentieth century warfare can probably be best understood as a series of blunders. Wasn't Norman Mailer's island battle resolved in the absence of the commanding officer, when a junior officer thought he was patching a gap in the line and wound up sweeping the whole island? It was probably a level below top brass that decided to send T-4 into the English Channel without escort. You can't blame Eisenhower for that. Who decided that it wasn't worth the trouble sending an air strike against a squadron of S-Boats lying a scant 90 miles across the water? We'll never know. There's no point looking for a scapegoat unless you want to blame the whole thing on Hitler. One commander didn't see it that way. Rear Admiral Don Moon commanded naval forces in Exercise Tiger. He commanded the same forces under the name Force U when they landed the VII Corps on Utah Beach on D-Day. After a successful landing on Utah, Admiral Moon was assigned to the Mediterranean to command the naval forces assaulting southern France. Shortly after boarding his flagship in Naples, Admiral Moon killed himself with a single shot to the head.

At daylight on April 28, about four hours after the S-Boat attack, we were sent into the beach on Slapton Sands. We unloaded, waited for the flooding tide and spent the night at anchor a mile off the beach. Next morning we headed up channel, across the mouth of Lyme Bay and, unknowing, over the sunken hulls of LSTs 507 and 571. The sea was calm. It had seen a lot of this kind of thing.

Ever since Glasgow we had known that we had more guns than we could man. Help was on the way. The morning after we anchored in Weymouth Roads, the signal tower called us to send a boat for our new crew members. As expected, they were all out of boot camp and, we discovered at the log-in, they all had names beginning with the letter "M." At first appearance the recruits didn't look any different from the crew. But, there *was* a difference. The youngsters who had left Chesapeake Bay a year ago were only 12 months older, but they now had 10,000 sea miles behind them, including two violent storms. They had been bombed, strafed and shelled and they had faced the underwater perils. There was a difference, all right. You could see it best in the eyes of the boot seamen beholding the veterans.

We also acquired a few young ensigns, fresh out of officer's school. It would be a while before they could stand a deck watch at sea but they could take over some of the OOD watches in port. At this time we acquired our own Mr. Roberts, an agreeable young man who was soon standing port watches. Roberts remains in my memory for one of his early port watches. We were anchored out and he was sending a liberty boat from the ship to a dock across the harbor.

The dock was clearly visible to Roberts and to me. We were both standing on the main deck. But it wasn't visible to the coxswain standing in the boat 15 feet below. Roberts repeatedly pointed to the dock and the coxswain repeatedly said he couldn't see it. Roberts began to show annoyance. "Right over there, goddam it," he shouted, pointing to the dock. At that moment an approaching seagull had Roberts' outstretched arm squarely in its sights. Direct hit. The bird laid its payload from the ensign's shoulder, down his sleeve to the single gold stripe. Never offend the sea gods.

At this point everybody from Hitler down to our newly acquired seamen knew that the cross channel invasion was imminent. We hoped that the command would give our new crewmen a chance to fire our guns at a moving target. It didn't happen.

Our next move was down the Channel back to the west coast of Lyme Bay. We moored in a small harbor called Torquay, about ten miles up the beach from Slapton Sands. Once again we sailed over the sunken hulls of LSTs 507 and 531. Torquay was a minor staging point for the assault on Normandy and the town was crowded with troops assembled to board the invasion fleet. It was there that I did my first and last stint as a policeman. The U.S. Army Military Police (MPs) are a trained unit; the Navy Shore Patrol (SPs) was a random group. When ordered by the port commander, a ship's captain would send a few men to headquarters where they were given arm bands, night sticks and brief instructions. I happened to be in visual range when our skipper received such orders and I found myself patrolling the streets of Torquay. I didn't carry a night stick; I was packing a Colt 45 and trying to look authoritative. I got the hang of it. I had two side men, an MP and an SP. We walked the crowded streets making ostentatious entries into each pub. Once inside we walked slowly down the bar, stopping at the far end to glare at the servicemen in the backroom. We didn't speak; we weren't spoken to. Back in the street we tried to give the pedestrians a similar display of the majesty of the law. It worked. We didn't arrest anyone.

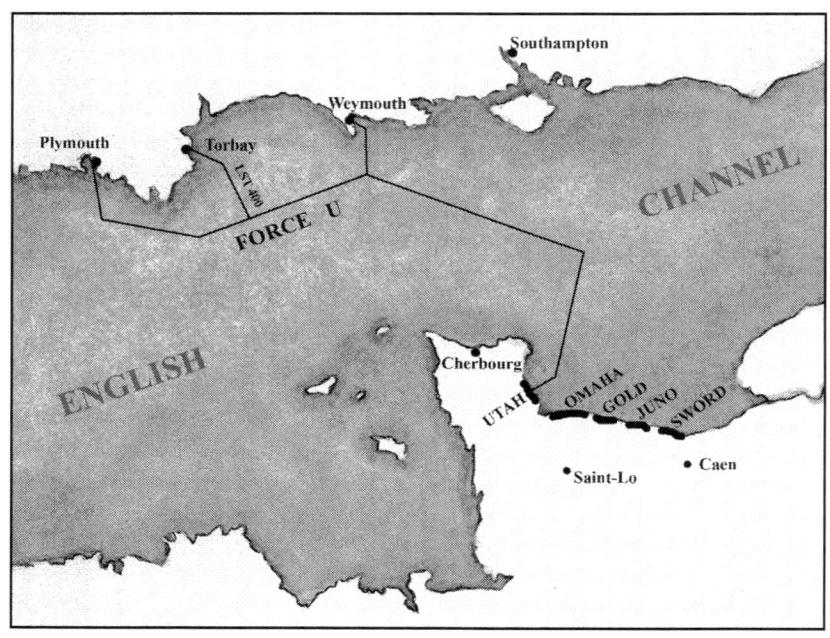

Assault Force U (Utah Beach)

CHAPTER 8

D-Day and Beyond

In June 1944 the Red Army destroyed the center of the German Army and moved into Poland and Finland. German officers tried to assassinate Hitler in July. The Allies invaded Normandy on June 6, freed Paris on August 25 and pushed east until December 19 when Germans counterattacked in the Battle of the Bulge. In June, U.S. Marines took Saipan in the Mariannas, 1,200 miles from Tokyo. In October, the U.S. fleet destroyed the Japanese Navy at Leyte Gulf.

The curtain went up on the morning of June 5. Here is an excerpt from our ship's log on that day:

0800–0922 Anchored as before. 0821 All preparations made for getting underway. 0827 Underway enroute anchorage to Utah Assault Area in accordance with Operation Order 1-44 of Commander Task Force Group 125-12 of June 2, 1944 in company with Torbay section of Convoy U-3, S.O.P.A. in USS Meredith *(DD726). OTC is Commander Task Group 125.15 in USS LST 691. Guide ship position 2-1. Ship's position 1-5. Captain at the conn. Navigator on the bridge, steaming on various courses and speeds to assume position in convoy. Generators #1 and #2 in use for steaming purposes. Made daily inspection of magazines. Conditions normal. Set Condition II.*

What that all means is that we hoisted anchor in Torbay and headed out into the Channel to meet the main section of the Utah assault force which started at Plymouth and was headed for Utah Beach in Normandy. That last line in the entry refers to powder magazines, not *The Saturday Evening Post.*

We steamed up the Channel all of June 5, staying in sight of the English coast. We were still headed east when I relieved the watch at 8:00 AM on June 6. At 10 AM the convoy wheeled right and headed for our target—Utah Beach. What happened next covers a range of activity so vast and complicated that it will never be fully comprehended. I can only relate what I actually saw, backed up by our ship's log and a few eyewitness recollections. The initial assault on the beaches had already begun. We were to learn that resistance on Utah Beach was light at the outset but that the Omaha assault waves were almost wiped out at the water's edge.

At 4:30 PM we were anchored off the French coast awaiting orders. By this time there were so many ships, anchored and passing, that I could see no semblance of order whatsoever.

Our flagship could reach us by radio, but I had no idea of where she was located. We were ordered into the Utah transport area where we anchored at 9:30 PM, still twilight in those northern midsummer waters.

June 6, 1944 stands out in world history as the day the Allies returned to western Europe. It stands out in the minds of LST 400 crewmen as the beginning of the longest stretch of hard work they put out in World War II. We were at grips with the enemy, threatened by fighter bombers, E-Boats, submarines and mines. Our task force lost ships to all those weapons. Those of us not manning guns were busy unloading assault cargo and personnel into a variety of vessels that came alongside. Similar landing craft returned from the beach with mixed groups of personnel. Eating was sporadic. Sleep was almost nonexistent.

As usual the first vehicles to leave our ship were the DUKWs. They were followed by trucks rolling down the ramp onto Rhinos, LCIs and LCTs. If the Navy jargon is getting a little heavy here, let me identify some of these craft.

USS **Nevada** *firing her forward 14" guns off Normandy, June 6, 1944: Our guns couldn't reply to the shore batteries but those on the USS* Nevada *could. We could see the shells, side by side, as they passed overhead. (National Archives: 80-G-252412)*

Rhino   a pontoon bridge powered by a large outboard motor

LCI   a 158-foot, flat-bottomed craft, designed to land 200 troops

LCT   a 119-foot, flat-bottomed craft, designed to land five tanks

DUKW   an amphibious truck with a watertight hull and a propeller

The goings and comings of these vehicles were highly irregular. The DUKWs made their way down the ramp and disappeared in a forest of ships in a choppy sea. Too choppy. We heard that only a few of them made it to the beach. When the last of the DUKWs had left we moved in closer to the beach where we could now make out the havoc wreaked on the beautiful Normandy shoreline. Tanks, trucks and landing boats were scattered like toys. Some were still unloading, some

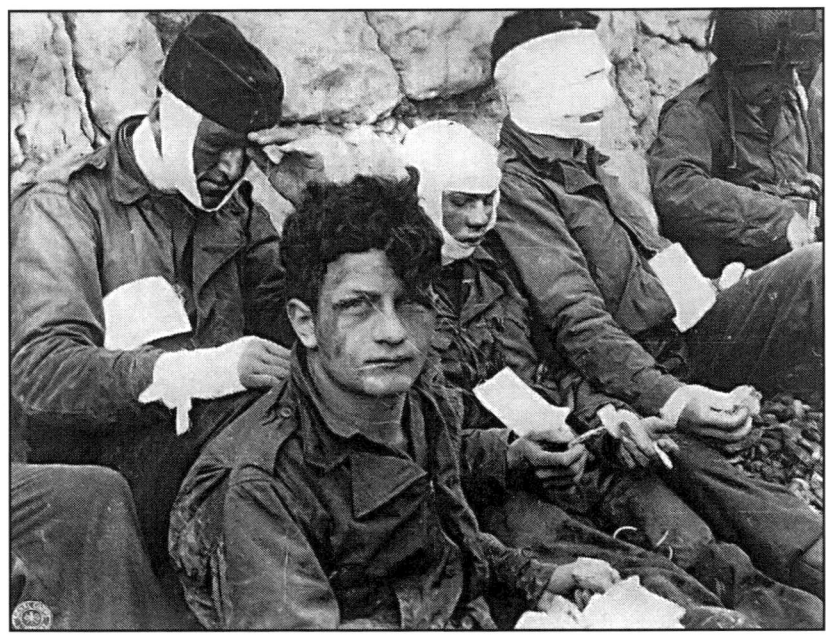

Omaha Beach Casualties: *do these faces reflect what they endured or what they saw? (National Archives: SC 189910)*

German Prisoners of War Awaiting Transport *(from Wikimedia Commons, public domain)*

were overturned, some were burning. But through the confusion we could see that men and machines were making progress inland. Just before sunset Rhino 220 approached our starboard side. We couldn't load or unload it over the side so I assume the Rhino crew was aboard to get a few meals from our galley and maybe a few hours' sleep in our bunks.

On the morning of June 7 the first LCT approached our bow. The bow-to-bow unloading went well in spite of the choppy sea. We spent the rest of the day discharging the usual cargo, but then a new development. In most of our Mediterranean landings we had returned from the beaches empty. This time we were going back to England with a mixed load of military personnel. An LCI brought us 70 Army glider pilots, all happy to be alive. In the early morning of June 6, their troop-laden gliders had been towed to the erratic landscape behind Utah Beach. Once turned loose by the tow-plane, it was the glider pilot's job to find an obscure landing strip in poor visibility. Many of them didn't make it. Next alongside was LCT 474 with a load of soldiers, but they weren't our soldiers. They were prisoners of war. These men didn't look like the members of the Wehrmacht that we had previously seen. There were about 200 of them and apparently they were conscripts from defeated eastern European countries. Some were in their teens; some were over forty. Such troops, I was told, surrendered easily. We settled them on the tank deck, saving the remaining bunks for our own troops. It's well we did. The next alongside was another LCI. This one brought us casualties, some able to walk. We had bunks for those guys.

Ships and landing craft passed us moving to and from the beach and some traveling parallel to the beach. Lord knows where they were going. At about 1:00 PM, one of those wanderers, a British freighter, struck a mine about 1,000 yards southeast of us. It sank rapidly. Survivors were pulled out of the water by empty landing craft returning from the beach. LCM 80 brought a small group of them to us. With the freighter survivors safely aboard we headed north. LST 400 had taken its first step on the road back to Europe.

LSTs Unload on Ebbing Tide. (National Archives: 80-G-252794)

Minesweeper USS **Tide** *Sinks After Hitting a Mine.* (National Archives: 80-G-651677)

Near Miss! LST Narrowly Escapes Shellfire from Utah Beach. (National Archives: SC 190276)

I took the conn at 8:00 PM as we sailed past Point Barfleur and out of the Baie de la Seine headed for England. Twilight had faded and we were steaming under a dark, overcast sky at 11:30 PM when I leaned over the speaking tube to caution a helmsman who had wandered a few compass points off course. When I lifted my head I was staring at the towering gray bow of a merchantman coming head-on. I called for full left rudder and prayed for the ship to answer. A slow swing to port had just begun as the ships slid past each other about twenty feet apart. We were so close that I could see the white face of a crewman staring down at me from his starboard wing. Apparently the northbound LST convoy and the southbound cargo ship convoy had sailed right through each other in the middle of the night. The odds against that happening without collision must be extremely high. I wouldn't want to try it again.

At 7:30 AM on June 9 we were in Weymouth harbor using our LCVPs to ferry the glider pilots, walking wounded and POWs into the dock. The more seriously wounded were held until we got into the hard where they could be picked up in ambulances. We'd had a good night's rest, but while we slept the Cherbourg nemesis struck again. The same squadron of S-Boats that had devastated Exercise Tiger sunk two LSTs off Point Barfleur, the same waters we had crossed the previous night. It was hard to believe. The U.S. Atlantic Fleet, His Majesty's Navy, The USAAF and the RAF could not contain nine S-Boats in Cherbourg harbor. Remember our old friend Joe LePage who saw the bombing of LST 158 at Licata, Sicily? Joe was in on this S-Boat fracas too. But this time he wasn't an observer, he was a victim. Let him tell it.

> *This is how I remember the attack from the E-Boats or their German torpedo boats. Have information that a German Lieutenant named Hoffman led the attack on us. We made the trip on June 6th and stayed out about six or seven miles and launched our 6 LCVPs (36' landing boats) as we were a six davit LST. We also were loaded on tank deck and topside with*

amphibious 36' ducks (DUKWSs) which were loaded with artillery guns. We launched them, if you remember, in six to eight foot seas and our LCVPs were to lead them into shore. One of our coxswains, Wallace W. Woodyard, reported that all overloaded ducks swamped and sank in the high seas. We left Omaha and arrived back in Plymouth.

We reloaded and went back to Normandy on the 8th of June and arrived about fifteen miles off the coast of Normandy in a five-ship convoy. Late on the evening of the 8th, HMS **Beagle** *saw our convoy and asked permission to escort us. The captain was Norman Munch. I was standing watch on the quad 40MM. I was the trainer. At 2:00 AM on the 9th I was talking to Donald Guilbeault who was from Providence R.I. when LST 314, who was about 300 yards forward of our port bow was hit by a torpedo and immediately burst into flames. I said to Guilbeault to keep eyes open or the same thing will happen to us. I no sooner got it out of my mouth than we got hit in the engine room and concussion picked me up in the air and blew me about 10 to 12 feet in air. Was dazed for a few seconds and a few seconds later we were ordered to abandon ship as trucks loaded with gas and ammunition were set on fire and the engine room and pressure to firefighting were down. I grabbed a Mae West life preserver and jumped overboard. The* **Beagle** *had picked up the E-Boats on radar and went after them. By the time the* **Beagle** *got back to us we had floated into a minefield and Captain Munch from the* **Beagle** *went into the minefield to pick us up. The water was 47 degrees as I had stood a watch in the engine room and one of our duties was to take the temperature of incoming seawater every half hour and the temperature of the seawater leaving the engines. When I went into the water at 2:05 I had foul weather gear on. The canvas outer layer had cellophane within the canvas as a wind blocker and, with an inner layer, this was the only thing that saved me from hypothermia as I wasn't picked up till about 5:30 in the morning. If HMS* **Beagle** *hadn't been with us, I'm sure the E-Boats would have sunk the other three ships in the convoy. I heard recently that the 496 was sunk the next night on the 10th of June as she hit a mine. We lost 68 men and never did find out how many soldiers were lost on the 324.*

Joe found himself right in the center of the sinking of LSTs 158, 314, and his own 376. If I'm ever again called on to invade enemy shores, I'll make it a point to stay as far away from Joe LePage as I can get.

The job ahead was enormous. A drive along any road in southern England led past fields crowded with guns, tanks, trucks and huge crates of god-knows-what. All had to be hauled over the beaches until the ports of Le Havre, Cherbourg and Brest were opened. Prior to D-Day we always had ample docking space but now it was a problem. We had to wait two days for our turn at Hard #3 in Portland. We were accommodated early on June 12 and by 2:30 PM we were on our way back to Utah. This time the turnaround was quick. By 6:00 PM the following day we were on our way back for another load. We had been unloading onto LCTs and other landing craft. This time we took a load of ammunition straight to Utah Beach. We grounded about 100 feet from the shoreline. In the Mediterranean that would have called for a pontoon bridge. Not at Utah. The English Channel has a 12-foot tidal range at Normandy. Even as we beached, the waterline was receding. A half hour later we were high and dry and I was able to walk along the ship's side to the stern where I stared *up* at the ship's propellers. Tidal range at Normandy was a significant factor. Landing craft (and ships) beached on an ebbing tide and stayed put until the returning tide lifted them off the sand.

LST 400 Grounded on Utah Beach
(U.S. Government, public domain)

LST 400, like the rest of the amphibs, crossed and recrossed the Channel constantly for the next six weeks. Allied forces were established on the mainland but progress inland was slow. Cherbourg was in Allied hands but needed a lot of work before it could be a serviceable harbor. Le Havre and Brest were still held by the Germans. Cherbourg harbor was eventually cleared of mines and otherwise rehabbed. Presumably the S-Boat squadron had been disposed of. By August 12 the port was open for business. By this time LST 400 had established its base at Southampton and started on a Southampton to Cherbourg shuttle that would last for months. We had been relegated to the mundane role of cargo ship, but I didn't hear of any yearning for the excitement of the beaches.

We took another step back from the rigors of war. We were allowed to spend one or two nights ashore for the first time since we left the States. Each time we moored in Southampton, one officer and twelve crewmen were given the privilege of catching the South West Railroad to Waterloo Station in London. It was a refreshing experience. In spite of the hardships of a sea blockade, German bombs and an inundation of GIs, the English seemed determined to hang on to a degree of civilization, confident that the barbarity would eventually end. We were all anxious to get to London where, we heard, big city life went on regardless of the V-1s and V-2s dropping around town.

Clarification:

V-1   called the "buzz bomb" by the servicemen. They were unmanned, jet-propelled, winged bombs, launched in France and designed to drop when their fuel was exhausted. V-1s were introduced in June 1944.

V-2   the first true rocket-bomb, launched from various sites on the mainland. It reached great altitudes and then dropped vertically on its target.

The V-1s didn't interfere much with our London holidays. We had grown accustomed to them in Southampton. We were

V-1 Flying Bomb *(from Bundesarchiv, Wikimedia Commons)*

V-2 Rocket Bomb *(from Bundesarchiv, Wikimedia Commons)*

occasionally able to fire at them. Their jet engine made a distinctive sound, hence "buzz bomb." When the buzz stopped, it was time to take cover.

London hotels, night clubs and theaters flourished, but the restaurants didn't have much to offer. It was in London that I first (and last) ate a pigeon. The fact that they called it a squab on the menu didn't change it much. It was in the theaters that Londoners excelled. Bombs or no bombs, London offered a greater repertoire than any other city in the war-torn world. I made only three trips to the city, but I was able to enjoy performances by Ralph Richardson, Laurence Olivier and John Gielgud in plays that included *Peer Gynt, Arms and the Man* and *Hamlet*.

The fact that I could enjoy the storied city on the Thames in its war-torn condition was due to the composure of the English people. By the time I got there, in the fall of 1944, Londoners had learned to live in their damaged city, crowded with their displaced countrymen and thousands of European refugees. Their greatest trial could well have been the swarms of American servicemen. The English and their former colonists had evolved along somewhat different lines. But the differences were largely superficial once we had dropped our preconceptions of one another. I expected the British to speak like characters out of P.G. Wodehouse. They had their preset ideas of how Yanks behaved. I was dancing with a WREN (Navy women's auxiliary) and our conversation was on introductory lines. She told me she was from some place in England that I had never heard of. Rather than trying to identify my obscure hometown, I told her I was from Chicago. Her eyes widened and she asked if I was carrying a gun. This wasn't in jest. Most Britishers of the time probably believed that Chicagoans wore shoulder holsters.

London was a delight if you could put the V-1s and V-2s out of mind. Think of taking a weekend break in Boston or San Francisco and having your pleasure-bent routine punctuated with a thundering explosion from time-to-time. The Brits didn't appear to feel threatened; why should we? The buzz bomb, while not exactly enjoyable was tolerable because you

Old Vic Theatre in London (from Caroline Ford, Wikimedia Commons 3.0)

could locate it by ear and then actually see it coming. The V-2 was another story. Falling from an altitude of over fifty miles, the bomb was traveling well above the speed of sound when it hit. Your first awareness was the explosion itself. That was followed by the whistling sound of the projectile passing through the air before it hit. Two of our crew traveled to London on their first overnight leave since leaving the States. They had just left Waterloo station when a V-2 exploded a quarter mile away. The two sailors, both veterans of Sicily, Italy and Normandy, decided that one of the south shore resort towns would be a better place to spend their leave. They caught the next train back to Southampton.

On August 23 we were called back into the war again. At the Southampton hard we took on an unusual and highly lethal load. Normally the fuel, food and ammunition we carried was packaged and loaded into trucks that rolled onto the tank deck at our home port and rolled off at our destination. This time it was piece work. We loaded 18,777 separate jerricans (5 gal) of high octane gasoline. The jerricans were delivered to us in trucks and unloaded one by one onto our tank deck. We set work details to help the Army with this onerous job. Still it took us more than a day to load. We secured the load and closed the bow doors at 10:00 PM. I was curious. We weren't going to haul piecemeal fuel cans to Cherbourg. By this time Cherbourg was well able to handle truck traffic. I went up to the office for a look at the orders. Our destination was St. Michel-en-Greve. Where the hell was that?

After the historic breakout at St. Lo, General Patton sent his tanks eastward toward Paris and westward toward the port city of Brest. Traveling at his characteristic speed, the general had outrun his fuel supply lines. He was within 20 miles of the much needed port of Brest and he was out of gas. At noon on August 25, according to the log, we were "standing down" the Solent. That's another one of those naval expressions that probably doesn't need explanation because the sound of the word says it all. It is applied to a ship moving through a confined passage of water. A ship standing down is heading out to sea. The confined passage in this case was the Solent, a stretch of water lying between the Isle of Wight and the coast of Hampshire. We crossed the English Channel that afternoon and were passing the Channel Islands of Alderney and Guernsey in the middle of the night.

St. Michel-en-Greve turned out to be a small town on the coast of Brittany about 30 miles northeast of Brest. Germans still held the port but our tanks were closing in. We moved into the beach just south of town. With the tide ebbing we could easily accommodate the empty Army trucks approaching our tank deck. Reversing our Southampton procedure we hand-loaded the gas cans, ship to truck. We started at 3:30 PM on the 26th, three trucks at a time, two crews to a truck (one loading, one resting). At midnight we had to break off loading and move the ship to adjust for the flooding tide. By 5:00 PM the next day, the 18,777[th] jerrican was on a truck heading for Patton's thirsty tanks and we were anchored offshore ready for our return to England.

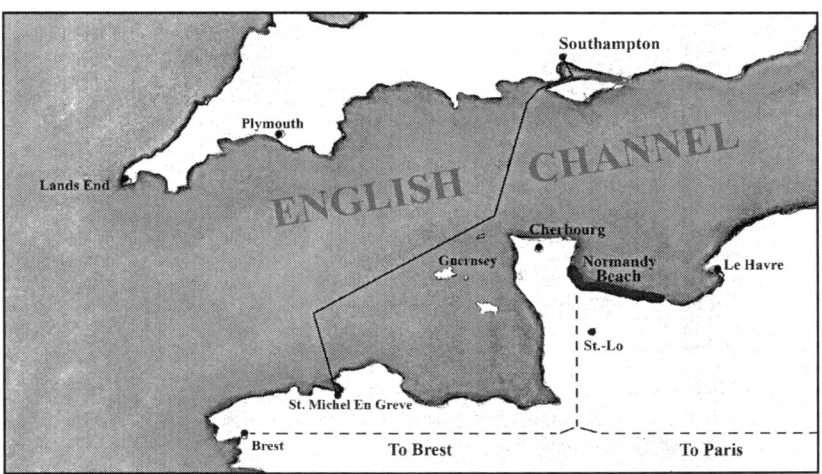

English Channel after D-Day

Back at Southampton we heard the happy news that Paris had been liberated. LST 400's war was changing: no Me109s, German artillery was hundreds of miles away and the S-Boat stronghold was finally overrun. While it was still possible for a U-Boat to slip into the Channel, damn few of them tried it. Mines continued to be a menace till the end of the war and well thereafter. Even our crew was beginning to change. Just before we left for St. Michel, Chief Commissary Steward Stevens and several crewmen got orders sending them back to the States.

The crew that had commissioned the new LST 400 had now been at sea for more than a year-and-a-half. The Navy's European task was winding down and the focus was shifting to Tokyo. The battle-hardened veterans of Sicily, Italy and Normandy were now needed as the nucleus for new crews being organized to land on Honshu. There was no letup for the Army, though. After the long armored run around Paris, the GIs were back to slogging it out with the Germans on their newly established defenses. On December 19, 1944, the Germans made a concentrated drive between American and British forces in the Ardennes forest. The ground they gained was soon known as "The Bulge."

Once again Army needs shaped our agenda. Shortly after the Bulge breakthrough we were called into the Southampton hard. The Army needed some supply for the Bulge battle—it wasn't gasoline. Whatever it was, we could get it to them faster if we hauled it up the Seine River. The Seine below Paris is very scenic and very twisted. It could have been a pleasure trip except for the mines. LST 6 learned this to her sorrow at few miles upstream from Le Havre. Our destination was Rouen. But first we had to pick up a river pilot at Le Havre. Our relations with

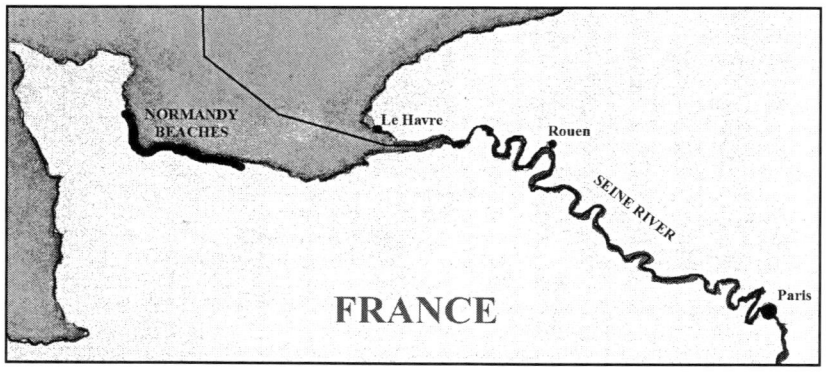

Seine River

M. Andre Pisibon got off to a bad start. Harbor pilots are very special people. They are taken aboard with respect and courtesy. When the pilot boat draws alongside, the ship's crew lowers a chain ladder. The pilot climbs the ladder and is assisted over the rail and greeted by the OOD. He is led to the bridge and introduced to the captain. M. Pisibon's reception was not up to standard. The chain ladder had been carelessly draped over the side in such a way that it crossed the exhaust vent from one of the auxiliary diesel engines. Neither the ship's crew nor the boat crew were aware of the situation until the pilot's head drew even with the exhaust vent. M. Pisibon could have retreated back down the ladder but, in his anger, he chose to climb through the exhaust gas, expelling a stream of Gallic curses that didn't subside until he reached the bridge. The pilot's English was only a little better than our French, but he managed to guide

LST 6, Sunk by Mine in Seine River, November 18, 1944 (U.S. Government, public domain)

our helmsman into the mouth of the Seine and up the winding river. The Seine River is not wide in its lower reaches and it was soon apparent that the guide was holding the ship too close to the riverbank. Too close for comfort. Dusk was approaching when the captain spoke to him:

"Aren't you staying too close to the shore?"

"I have to," replied M. Pisibon, "that's about as far as I can see."

"All engines stopped," called the skipper, resuming command.

We soon found a quiet stretch of water for anchoring. M. Pisibon joined us for dinner in the wardroom but the conversation was strained.

The City of Rouen is famous for its cathedral and for the burning of Joan of Arc. Security precluded sightseeing and we were too late to help Joan. We beached downstream from the town. There was no hard there but the mud bank was fairly stable and with the use of some heavy planking we were able to unload. The downriver trip was uneventful and we dropped M. Pisibon at Le Havre in mid-afternoon. This time we placed the ladder well clear of the exhaust vent.

Back at Southampton we slipped back into our cargo ship routine, but this time with a twist. In early January we pulled into a Southampton hard where a truck-mounted welding machine pulled onto our tank deck. It was followed by a flatbed truck loaded with rails, the kind freight trains run on. The flotilla commander hadn't told us about this. No matter. The welders went to work and soon had three lines of European style (narrow gauge) railroad tracks welded to our deck. I was wondering how they would get freight cars aboard when another truck pulled up with a three-way switch. The switch was welded to the ramp and we were ready to load three track loads of freight cars on our tank deck. An engine appeared pushing six loaded gondolas and then six more and soon we had a freight train crossing the English Channel. The switch/dock was ready at Cherbourg and the following day we were back at Southampton having completed our first round trip of rail service. Did I say that LSTs could haul anything? If required, we could have removed the rails and hauled a load of bulk horseradish to Burma the next day. No such exigency arose and we hauled rail cars from Southampton to Cherbourg for the rest of the war.

LST 400 Unloading Rail Cars at Cherbourg (U.S. Government, public domain)

The Wehrmacht's push into the Ardennes had been stopped at Bastogne but driving them back to the Rhine was a slow, painful struggle. There was a lot of dying to be done yet. LST 400, however, had slipped into a less hazardous routine. Our Southampton/Cherbourg rail shuttle service was largely free of enemy harassment. In the port of Cherbourg we unloaded rail cars a few hundred yards from the piers where our old foe the Raven used to moor. Minefields had been swept from the Channel for the most part, U-Boats were blocked out and the Luftwaffe was just an unpleasant memory. But we still had to deal with the sea, at times sparkling under a bright sun and again driven into monstrous waves by a relentless wind. In March 1945 we met a head-on gale on a night run to Cherbourg. I had the midwatch and was having a helluva time staying on course as the gale swung our high, round bow from side-to-side. The admiralty now felt secure enough to place lighted buoys in the Channel. Shortly after I took the conn at midnight we struggled past Buoy E. At 2:30 AM we passed it again.

After clearing one Channel gale, I looked up from the tank deck to see sunlight streaming through a crack in the main deck. The crack opened about a half inch and then closed as the ship flexed its way through the water. I had heard of badly loaded ships breaking in half in heavy weather and I shot up the ladder to tell the skipper he had a broken ship. There was nothing we could do about it except stay the course for Southampton, six hours away. This we did, heaving a sigh of relief as we slipped into the lee of the Isle of Wight. We notified the flotilla commander, fully expecting a week in dry dock. He didn't even reply to our cry of distress. When it came our turn to load, we were called into the hard where a truck came aboard, fitted with a welding machine and carrying a dozen steel plates. While we loaded, the plates were welded over the crack and we were ready for sea. We were to learn that more LSTs than not had cracked their main decks in storms.

On March 8 we were told that the U.S. Army had crossed the Rhine at Remagen bridge. I don't know if that crossing was

Routine Watch in Port: Bosun-of-the-Watch, A.A. Braginton, BM 1/c, Middle Village, NY (at left); Officer-of-the-Deck, Gene Jaeger, Lieut., Geneva, IL (at right) (courtesy of the author)

a great tactical advantage or not. It sure was a great psychological advantage. Across the Rhine! Now we had that sonofabitch with the pimpy mustache right where we wanted him.

The curtain was coming down on the Navy's performance in European waters. Our crew continued to leave in stages. Every few weeks we'd get orders sending four or five of our originals back to the States for leave and reassignment. By mid-March less than half of the plank owners (on board at commissioning) remained. In early April, at a routine 8:00 AM muster, Captain Lyden announced that he had been relieved and that a new skipper would be on board that afternoon. The crew was shocked. Their captain was leaving them; the "old man" who took over in the Chesapeake when they didn't know how to lace their shoes, the man who led them into their first battle that stormy night in Sicily, the man who maneuvered them through the white fog while escaping the beach at Salerno. No farewell speech; no personal good-byes. Late that afternoon, the captain walked down the dock, climbed into a staff car and we never saw him again.

Another dramatic exit soon followed. On April 12 our commander-in-chief died. The crew was never very vocal about their feelings for their captain or their president but it was impossible for them to have done what they did in the past 26 months without confidence in their leaders: Charles J. Lyden and Franklin D. Roosevelt. The new skipper was a guy named John O'Brien and the new president was a guy named Harry S. Truman. Never heard of either one of them. I was aware of the crew's unease but nothing was said out loud until I was approached by a young BM 2/c who seemed embarrassed to say what was on his mind. "Mr. Jaeger, don't you think it would be a good idea for Mrs. Roosevelt to run the country until this goddam war is over?"

The new skipper took over and I became the executive officer. We may have made a few more trips to Cherbourg; I'm not sure. The European part of World War II ended on May 8, 1945.

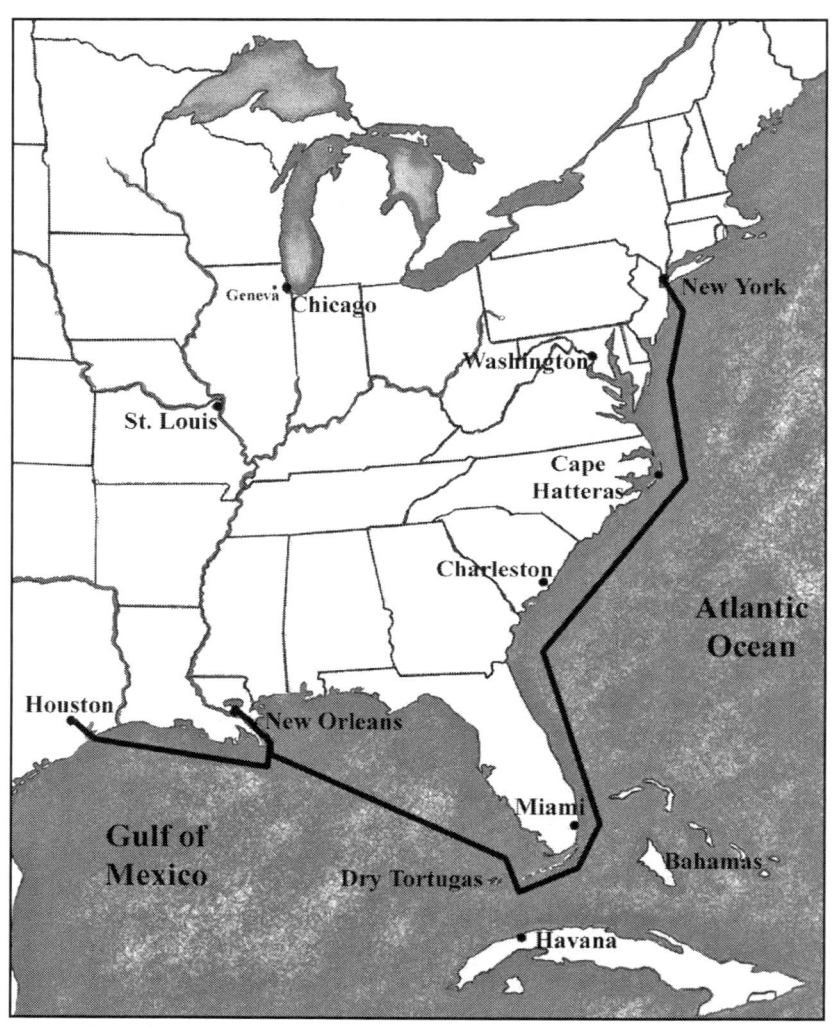

Final Journey Aboard LST 400

CHAPTER 9

Stateside

On May 8, 1945, Germany surrendered to American/British forces in the west and to Soviet forces in the east. The horrors of Auschwitz and Buchenwald were revealed to a stunned world. Some Allied troops were assigned occupation duty, the majority was ordered home. The struggle for Okinawa, only 350 miles from Japan, had begun.

The urgency of 1943 was now reversed. The flow of arms and men was now westward.

War-weary servicemen wanted to go home and the public clamored for their return. Again, the means of transportation were strained. Every ship or aircraft headed west was loaded with servicemen. LST 400 carried a group of Dutch marines and a contingent of U.S. Army Air Force survivors of downed aircraft. These lucky-to-be-alive airmen were just released from German prison camps. I recall their amusement in the retelling of one of their group diving out the door of a burning plane shouting "what town is this?" I drew some of their attention as the executive officer with the big, red mustache. After shaving it off, I walked into the wardroom to be greeted with "he's just a kid."

We had ample room now and the Dutch marines were comfortably housed two bunks to a rack, not four like our Army brothers on invasion trips. One of the marines complained to his sergeant that he had been robbed by one of our black gang. The sailor was accused of lifting the sleeping marine's wallet while on his way to a night watch in the engine room. I had the marine and his sergeant and the sailor and his chief brought to my cabin. It was pretty clear the sailor was guilty but he denied it. I didn't want to have to prove the charges at a captain's mast, so we worked out a deal: the sailor hadn't stolen any money, but he agreed to give it back. The marine got his money, the sailor kept his record clean and I was spared a petty squabble marring my homeward bound euphoria.

The Atlantic behaved and we had a quiet crossing. About halfway across the commodore called for an inspection and confiscation of all weapons. Between passengers and crew we turned up enough guns to start an insurrection. They ranged from highly prized German Lugers to regular Army rifles. I don't know how they got them aboard. One kid even had an anti-tank gun, a high caliber rifle with a long barrel resting on a bipod. I managed to make off with a 30-caliber carbine. It's still in the family somewhere.

Late in May, the Cape Charles and Cape Henry lighthouses appeared. I don't know which we saw first. It didn't matter.

Cape Henry Lighthouse (U.S. Navy, public domain)

Cape Charles Lighthouse (National Park Service, public domain)

Both were firmly grounded in the United States. We crossed the Chesapeake and anchored in Hampton Roads but it wasn't much of a homecoming. The signalman brought me a message saying that we had been refused pratique. A helluva note. It's bad enough being refused but it's worse if you don't know what you're being deprived of. I read the message, nodded knowingly and when the signalman was out of the office I dove for the dictionary. We had been denied health clearance. Apparently the pharmacist's mate had been in communication with a doctor on the flagship about a sick marine. The mate's description of the symptoms suggested meningitis to the doc who forwarded the diagnosis to the medics at Norfolk Navy Base. We were quarantined, for God's sake. Welcome home! We swung at anchor for a few days. Hampton Roads hadn't changed in the past two-and-a-half years. The base commander eventually sent boats to take the Dutch marines ashore but our crew and our airmen guests were still confined to ship. The day after the marines left we got our orders. Without so much as putting a foot ashore we were ordered to set sail for New York harbor, much to the delight of our largely New England crew. The flyboys seemed to like the idea, too.

Ambrose Lightship in New York Harbor (U.S. Coast Guard, public domain)

We followed the same route up the coast we'd traveled in 1943. This time the lights of Atlantic City glowed cheerfully and Ambrose Light was flashing a welcome as we swung into lower New York Bay and headed up the Hudson River. I recall that we tied to a pier somewhere north of 42nd Street. For some reason native New Yorkers call this stretch the North River even though it runs down the west side of Manhattan Island. Forget

Hampton Roads, New York was home. Our stay was brief. We sent our easterners for a short leave home and sent our air force buddies on their way. The best I could manage was a phone call home from Jack Dempsey's restaurant.

Our travel agent godfather was writing our orders again. This time he rang the bell. We were ordered to proceed to Algiers; no, not back to the Med, this Algiers was in Louisiana, across the river from New Orleans. Hard to beat that. If you had just finished two years of warfare in Europe and were slated to do another stretch in Japan, what place would you choose for a short lay over. New Orleans would have to be high on your list. It was at the top of mine. We managed to get the crew back aboard with no AOLs (absent over leave) and we pulled out into the Hudson, pilot aboard and New York's magical skyline gliding past. We dropped the pilot, rounded Sandy Hook and headed back down the coast. This time it was different. No convoy. The U-Boats had all surrendered and there were no Me109s, no tanks and no artillery on the friendly Jersey shore. USS LST 400 was sailing free and clear. Not a ship within five miles of us. Four hour sea watches weren't a burden. If the sea behaved and you could keep your mind off Japanese beaches, this wasn't a bad way to go.

Even Hatteras was quiet as we sailed by. I held the ship close to the Florida coast to avoid the full seven-knot, northbound current in the Straits of Florida. If we'd met that current head on with our nine-knot cruising speed it would have taken us a full day to travel 50 miles. We followed the Keys around to Dry Tortugas where we left the sight of land and set out across the Gulf of Mexico for the mouth of the Mississippi River. Another pleasure cruise. The Gulf was calm and sunny but we did sight waterspouts which are honest-to-god whirlwinds but are as harmless as the "dust devils" we used to see on the Midwest prairie. As we moved into the mouth of the big river we saw the pilot boat approaching us from, (where else?) Pilottown. I was surprised to learn that we had a long upriver run to make. New Orleans is more than 100 miles from the Gulf of Mexico.

The Mississippi River delta is formed in hundreds of square miles of topsoil that has washed down from the uplands over the centuries. It is largely overgrown with forest running right

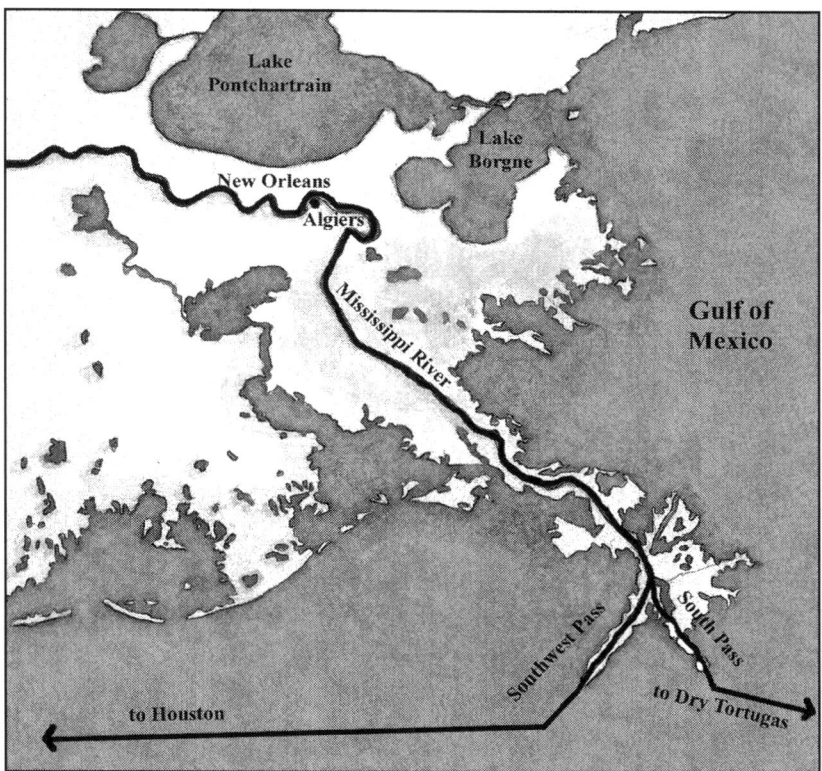

Mississippi River Delta

to the riverbank. LST 400 was destined to leave its mark on that forestland. We were about forty miles upstream from the Gulf when the pilot called for ten degrees left rudder. The helmsman responded and the rudder moved ten degrees left—and stayed there. The jammed rudder was due to a hydraulic airlock (a long story). The ship's bow began its swing to the west riverbank. The skipper had seen the airlock before, so he immediately relieved the pilot. The procedure called for backing down on all engines, which he did. It also called for dropping the bow anchor, which he also did—or tried to. The anchor detail in the fo'c'sle (forecastle) was standing by, ready for just such an emergency. The talker wearing headphones (he was 200 feet from the bridge) happened to be an apprentice seaman we had just picked up in New York a few weeks back. The bridge talker and the fo'c'sle talker exchange went something like this:

Bridge: "Let go the bow anchor."

Fo'c'sle: "What?"

Bridge: (getting excited) "Let go the bow anchor."

Fo'c'sle: "Bow anchor manned and ready."

The riverbank was coming up fast and the skipper was shouting at the bridge talker:

Bridge: "I know it's manned and ready; let the damn thing go."

Fo'c'sle: "What?"

By this time the bosun of the anchor detail was aware of the agitation on the bridge. He grabbed the headset from the talker. The riverbank loomed.

Bosun: "Fo'c'sle aye."

Bridge (screaming): "Let go the bow anchor."

Bosun: "Aye, aye."

In sequence, the bosun called to his detail: "let her go," a seaman swung a sledge hammer which opened the pelican hook releasing the anchor chain, the anchor slid down the hawse pipe, the ship hit the mud bank, the anchor landed in a tree. Of course, I logged the incident: the jammed rudder, the skipper taking control and the ship running aground. But I think I left out that part about the anchor landing in a tree. Washington brass doesn't have to know everything. Besides, we were just outside New Orleans, the Big Easy, where nobody gets upset about things like anchoring in a tree.

Satellite View of New Orleans (NASA, public domain)

Crowded, noisy, flamboyant Bourbon Street on a spring night was dreamland after the gritty world we had been living in. Tourist trap, sure. But so is St. Peter's. I had always flaunted my superior taste in pop music without really having had the opportunity to hear much of it. I praised primitive jazz and derided Guy Lombardo. In New Orleans I found substance for my dilettante posturing. The music was great. I have returned to New Orleans as often as possible. The last time was four months before Katrina.

I caught the last ferry boat to Algiers the night before our departure. LST 400 was about to travel the last leg on its odyssey. The same pilot who stood by in amused wonder while we anchored in a tree, was about to take us back down the river. He left us at the mouth of the Southwest Passage and we pointed our bow at Galveston. We headed up the Houston Ship Canal to the shipyards where we would be transformed from an Atlantic landing ship to a Pacific landing ship. We wanted to continue enjoying our homeland with no regard for the days ahead, but the shipyard managers kept the Rising Sun before our eyes for our entire stay. Our radar was being upgraded to better scan *Japanese* shorelines; new guns were added to fire at *Japanese* aircraft; the Navy kicked in with a complete set of charts for *Japanese* waters.

There was little for us to do while shipyard workers swarmed our decks. At headquarters I saw an attractive girl working over a filing cabinet. After a few preliminaries, I suggested dinner. She agreed, naming a time and place. Great, I hadn't had a date since Southampton and I showed up at the restaurant on the dot. So did she—with her teenage sister. It was an evening of good music and pleasant conversation. No romance. I intended to try again but the next morning my orders came: take 30 days' leave and report to Great Lakes Naval Station for reassignment. Reassignment? That meant my days on LST 400 had come to an end. Over half the crew was reassigned. I still wonder about the farewells. There weren't any. These men had lived together under the most trying circumstance for the past two-and-a-half years and their partings in Houston would be permanent. But the farewells were casual. I didn't see much handshaking or hear any promises to write and, certainly, no embracing. Men didn't do that in 1945. I caught a night flight to Chicago. I recall flying above a thunderstorm as we passed over St. Louis. I killed a little time at Chicago's Midway Airport and then took the El downtown. A short walk brought me to the Northwestern Station and I boarded a train to Geneva. Ithaca!

Hiroshima before the Bombing *(U.S. Department of Defense, public domain)*

Hiroshima A-Bombed. *(National Archives, U.S. Army, public domain)*

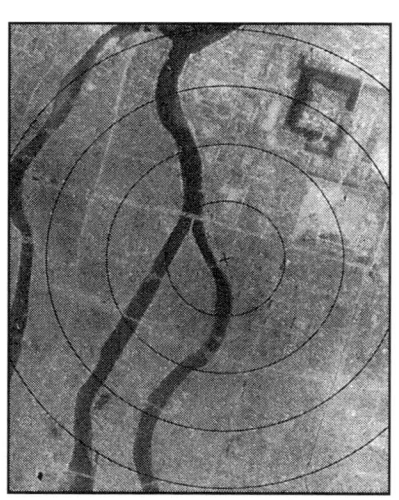

Hiroshima after the Bombing. *(Government of Japan, public domain)*

Chapter 10

Anti-Climax

The United States was torn between celebrating victory in Europe and mourning its dead. The country expected to pay a terrible price in the occupation of Japan. Military production was at a peak.

On August 7, 1945, I came down to a late breakfast. My sister, Bette, was having a last cup of coffee before leaving for work. "Take a look at this," she said, holding up the morning *Chicago Tribune*. The headline said that the USAAF had wiped out the Japanese port city of Hiroshima with a single bomb. I took this to be a technical breakthrough for the munitions industry. I was more gratified than horrified. I vaguely saw the new weapon as an instrument that might save my own skin by forestalling the invasion of Japan. There was a growing feeling in the armed forces that if you stayed at this game long enough you would get your lumps. I had four landings under my belt and the odds were shortening. An attempt to land on Kyushu would be crowding my luck. I thought of the new bomb as merely the latest gain in our destructive power. We had been destroying European cities with "blockbusters" so now we were moving up to "city busters." My understanding of the full horror of nuclear fission came later. I waved to Bette as she left and flipped to the sports section. The Cubs were in first place. This could be their year.

A few days later the Air Force dropped a second A-Bomb on Nagasaki and World War II came to an end. Geneva rejoiced that its men deployed in the Pacific would be coming home.

The casualty list was already far too long. This town of 4,200 had 26 names on the Honor Roll (obituary) on the city hall lawn. To that list I could add the same number of high school and college friends. We became hardened to death notices. They were everyday occurrences on this planet in the years 1939–1945.

I spent my leave loafing on the front porch of the family home and hanging out with the European vets beginning to trickle home. One was Billy Smith, the kid next door, now Lieut. William Smith, USA. Bill was wounded at Anzio and now walked with a crutch. His military days were over, but he was able to join me in roaming northern Illinois after sundown. He also joined me on a trip to Great Lakes where the commandant of the 12th Naval District had orders for my next duty. Bill consoled me on the way home as I read my new assignment. Those bottle-spinners at the Bureau of Personnel hadn't changed in the last three years. Instead of acknowledging my two-year effort in Europe with a soft berth in the U.S. for the remaining months, they assigned me to the USS AKA *Sidonia*, whatever the hell that was. It wasn't a warship. As a matter of fact, I didn't know what an AKA was. It turned out to be a freighter. I thought the Merchant Marine had all the freighters but apparently the Navy had a few. Freighters haul freight; they haul it over huge expanses of ocean, sometimes out of sight of land for weeks. Some old sailors love that kind of life. Not this old sailor. I did love sailing on those seas that bordered the white cliffs of Dover or the rock bound coasts of Maine, and on those that afforded ports of call such as London, New York and New Orleans. Looking at 360 degrees of horizon day after day was not my style of seafaring.

My orders told me to report to the *Sidonia* by FAGTRANS, Navy jargon for "first available government transport." The transportation to my ship was to be provided by the commandant of the 12th Naval District in San Francisco. That sounded good. I loved port cities (still do). I still had ten days' leave and I came up with the idea of touring the lands west of the Mississippi. I asked Bill Smith if he wanted to come along. Bill was game. Now I needed a car. New cars wouldn't be on the market for a few years but used ones were available. I was told I could buy one locally and make a killing selling it in San Francisco. I was also told that I could get the best deal on a used car at an auction, so I headed for one on Chicago's south side near Comiskey Park, at that time home of the White Sox. The auction was in progress so I joined a group of professional buyers following the auctioneer around the car lot. When I thought I had the auctioneer's chant figured out I threw up my hand and made a bid. The auctioneer broke off his chant and with a pained expression told me that he had passed that number two bids back. A half hour later I laid down $845 and drove home in a 1939 Chevy coupe. The next problem was gasoline. I was aware that the supply of gas, along with meat, sugar and other commodities was controlled by the government through stamp books. The American people responded well to the rationing system with a minimum of corner-cutting. Hell, it wouldn't be America if no one was trying to beat the system. I was invited to dinner by friends of the family and the host told me in a conspiratorial whisper that he got the steak from a wholesale packer in Hampshire. But I didn't need the black market for the gasoline to get me to San Francisco. I flashed my orders and was given stamps for an ample supply of gas.

We enjoyed the trip. There were no interstate highways at the time and, given the sparse traffic, no need for them. Two-lane concrete roads took us through fields of ripening corn and through the cities of Des Moines and Omaha. I had trouble accepting the name "Omaha" as a city when the whole world knew it was a bloody strip of sand on the Normandy coast. We drove through wheat fields, grassland and eventually the foothills of the Rockies as we approached Cheyenne. We spent the nights in tourist cabins, rectangular wooden frame structures housing two bunks and little more. Showers and toilets were available at the bathhouse. Motels were a thing of the future.

We crossed the Rocky Mountains, the flats west of Salt Lake and then the Sacramento valley on our way to the city by the

Golden Gate Bridge from Seaward (from Aaron Logan, Wikimedia Commons, 1.0)

bay. Today I visit big cities like a raw tourist, staring, mouth agape, at the tall buildings, riding sightseeing buses and taking harbor tours. Not then. In New York it had to be 52nd Street or the Village. In New Orleans it was the French Quarter. I don't recall if San Francisco had a particularly hep neighborhood. If it did we found it. Bill and I did acknowledge the existence of cable cars and the Golden Gate Bridge but we concentrated on the night scene. I discovered the legendary trumpeter Bunk Johnson, blowing in a small club near the bay. I loved SF. The only drawback was waiting in block-long gas lines.

I would have enjoyed an indefinite stay in San Francisco but my leave time was running out and I had to get on with the FAGTRANS. Bill caught a train for Chicago and I sold my car for $830, a net loss of $15. I approached Com 12 hoping that my new ship was somewhere on the coast.

"Where's the USS *Sidonia*," I asked the duty officer. He shuffled through papers; no computers then.

"It's headed for Guiuan," he told me.

"Where's Guiuan?"

"A port on Leyte."

I'd known about Leyte alright. Leyte Gulf was the site of history's last full dress naval battle. It was there in October 1944 that the U.S. Navy put the Japanese Navy out of war for keeps. It was the battle that enabled us to put General McArthur and his cameramen ashore.

"OK. Put me on the first flight to the Philippines."

A possible layover in Manila sounded good but that was not to be. The first *flight* to the Philippines turned out to be the

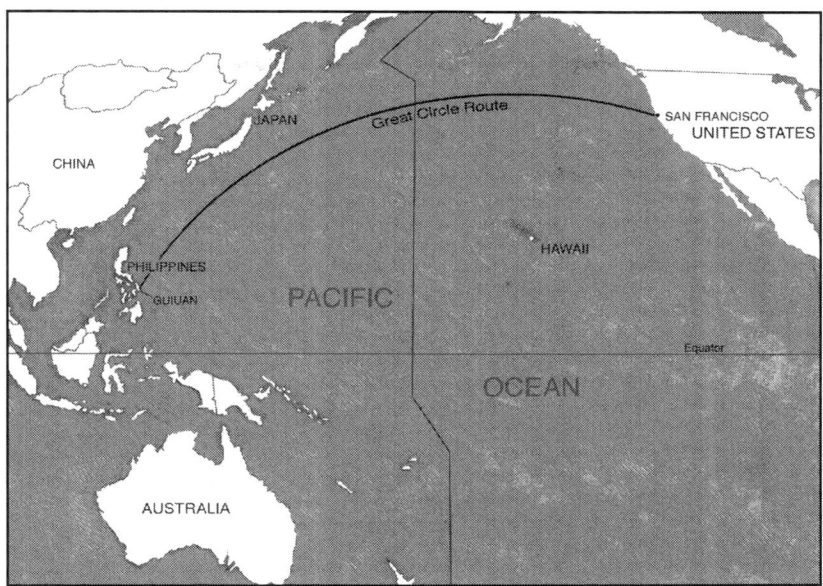

The Great Circle Route from San Francisco to Guiuan, Philippines

SS *Mormac Dove*, an old rust-bucket merchantman belonging to the Moore–McCormac line. Crossing the entire Pacific Ocean by ship was bad enough, but this wasn't even a Navy ship. I was shipped to the islands like cargo on a commercial freighter.

The sightseeing was great leaving San Francisco Bay. We passed the Golden Gate and watched the rugged northern California shoreline fade away on our starboard quarter. I was told to watch for seals on the Farallon Islands' rocky coasts but we were too far away. Past the Farallons we faced about 5,000 miles of open water. The California mainland disappeared and we began to roll. It was a moderate roll that stayed with us most of the way across the Pacific. A rolling sea is not hard to live with. If you were fortunate enough to have a porthole in your cabin, the subdued sound of water rushing by and the gentle side-to-side motion of the ship would rock you to sleep in minutes.

After getting assigned to a cabin and locating the wardroom (dining room) I wandered up to the bridge, feeling sure that the ship's mates would be delighted to hear from an old salt from the Mediterranean and the North Atlantic. I was quick to sense that these merchant marines had not only sailed those waters but all the other oceans on the globe as well. I noticed we were steering a course slightly north of due west which would seem odd to a landsman looking at a flat projection map of the Pacific. That would show the Philippine Islands to be definitely southwest of San Francisco. The northwest trajectory makes sense when you plot it on a globe and it becomes clear that you are sailing around the earth's hump rather than over it. Next time you see a globe, get a piece of string and try it.

My roommate was George Nussbaum, a Presbyterian chaplain from South Dakota. George made a mild appearance and he surprised me when I found out he was a sharp card player. We were soon involved in a non-stop, trans-Pacific game of cribbage. The game covered our waking hours. I remember the routine: "…fifteen two, fifteen four and a pair for GO." Then, a glance at the clock to see how long till lunch. We'd break the routine with a walk around the deck where, with a little luck, we might catch sight of a seagull or a porpoise. If you spend any length of time with a man of the cloth in the military, you eventually light on a comfortable form of address, one that recognizes his status but isn't too formal. Most servicemen addressed all chaplains, inaccurately, as "Padre." My roommate and I were soon using first names.

The Pacific Ocean is the most barren piece of the universe this side of Saturn. We didn't see as much as a reef between North America and the East Indies. Sometime in the first week of October I climbed a short way up the mast and made a historic landfall. It was the island of Samar in the Philippines. Soon we were anchored offshore of my destination, Guiuan. When I bid the chaplain good-bye, I claimed the cribbage championship of the North Pacific. He disputed this and insisted on a playoff. It never happened.

The Navy base at Guiuan consisted of newly constructed two-story, wooden frame buildings lying between the sandy beach and the surrounding jungle. I was assigned to a bottom bunk in a large dormitory and given a pass to the chow line. I then set about my business. In my long sea journey (nearly three weeks) I had almost forgotten why I had come to this godforsaken place. Of course, I was looking for the *Sidonia*. The duty officer was a redheaded guy with a distant stare. I never knew when I had his attention. His stare became even more distant when I asked him about the *Sidonia*. He not only did not know where the ship was, he had never heard of it. He added, with a "don't bother me" air, that he didn't have enough radio power to search the whole Pacific. I had the feeling that with the Naval Observatory at his disposal, he couldn't have found his belt buckle. He did tell me I could check in at his office each morning. I wandered back to the mess hall, tired and depressed.

A night's sleep helped, but I got up the next morning wondering what I was going to do on this desert island while I waited for my ship. I was in for a pleasant surprise. After breakfast I stepped out on the mess hall porch to see a bunch of guys moving around in a fenced field. A baseball game! I joined them while they were choosing up sides. They were just short of two full teams so I and another straggler were asked to play. I was no better than average at our national pastime and some of the players looked pretty good, particularly a catcher whose name I later ran across on a minor league roster. They had openings at third base and left field. I turned down third base because, while I had a pretty good arm, I was shaky fielding ground balls on the short hop. I went one-for-four at bat and managed to hold my own in the outfield. I was asked to come back the next day—and the next. But there was more good news in store. I walked back to the barracks with the second-baseman, a guy from Lorain, Ohio. He asked me to join a poker game at the base hospital. I was beginning to like Guiuan. I lost a couple of bucks that afternoon but I did meet Jim Brutz, a classmate and a right tackle at Notre Dame. I don't recall why Jim was hospitalized but it wasn't serious. He was out in a few days.

During the evening there was the officer's club and, with the war over, no shortage of beer. No women, of course. There were a few nurses at the hospital and native girls living with their families nearby. But this was a man's world. If you couldn't make it on baseball, beer and poker, it was a hard way to go.

The year wore on through October, November and December. What a routine: a late breakfast, a brief warm up followed by a ten o'clock baseball game and then lunch. The dining hall had a lounge supplied with old magazines like a dentist's office. Good enough to while away an hour or two before the poker game. Next a little letter writing, dinner, two hours at the officer's club and so to bed. Every other day I'd go to headquarters to face the vacant stare. He not only had no news of the *Sidonia*, he seemed to have trouble recalling who I was.

The same routine with the same bunch of guys day after day can lead to friction. It did with me and a member of our poker group. We irritated each other starting with our first hand of five-card stud. Casual day-to-day needling led to open conflict one day when I decided to leave the poker game early. I was four bucks ahead and this annoyed him. He wanted to know what I had on my agenda that was so important as to require my walking out of a poker game when I was ahead. I replied in kind and went about my important business. We picked up where we left off that night at the club. I made a few cutting remarks that bothered him and he said so. I told him I didn't know what I had said to annoy him but, whatever it was, I'd be happy to repeat it. That did it. His first shot hit the top of my head and I replied with a blow to the neck. Our buddies moved in like hockey linesmen and the battle was over. A lieutenant commander chewed me out for conduct unbecoming an officer. End of incident.

There's no winter in the Philippines so my holiday routine ran right through February. Near the end of the month I made a routine call on Stone Face. This time the conversation took a different turn. The *Sidonia* had reappeared. "Where?" I asked him. "San Francisco," he replied. I asked for an immediate transfer to the States, and to my surprise he sprang into action. I guess he was tired of my confronting him every two days. He buzzed the Bureau of Personnel who replied in an amazingly short time that I was now under the command of the Eighth Fleet and I would have to report to the commander for reassignment. And where would I find Com 8. The redhead was all business now. He shuffled his papers, "the commander of the Eighth Fleet is now aboard the USS *St. Paul* in Shanghai." Wrong direction. I wanted to go east but my starting point would have to be on the Chinese mainland. Another job for FAGTRANS which this time turned out to be a destroyer scheduled to leave for Shanghai the next day.

After all the tubs I had been riding for the past year, I was now on a ship-of-the-line. I caught a liberty boat out to the destroyer and the captain himself happened to be at the gangway.

He didn't have any chores for me on the run to Shanghai, but he said I was free to wander about the ship. I started out with the bridge but soon found that destroyers are controlled from a compartment just aft of the wheelhouse, called the C.I.C. (combat information center). This darkened room held a large, horizontal plotting board, illuminated from below. The board had a compass rose printed on its face and it was used to plot data flowing in from the sonar (sub detection), radar (surface and air detection) and the gyro compass. I spent hours in the C.I.C. and on the bridge as we sailed between Taiwan and Okinawa headed for the mouth of the Yangtze River.

The rigors of war were fading and the civilians-turned-sailors were beginning to chafe under military discipline. Some guys just weren't cut out for this sort of life. One of the destroyer officers gave me an example of this war-weariness in an incident involving a task force operating near the Philippines. The task force commander was dissatisfied with radio circuit discipline which required radio operators to get permission to use a specific circuit, to stick to brief transmissions of official business and to avoid all superfluous conversation. The commander had his deputy call all communications officers to their radio phones for a lecture on circuit discipline. The lecture was delivered as a diatribe in which the deputy repeatedly referred to the commander by his code name, which was "Flabby."

"Flabby has become aware that several ships have...."

"Flabby calls all CO's attention to Section IIA...."

"Flabby hereby instructs all communication personnel to...."

"All breaches in circuit discipline will be reported to Flabby. Out."

All circuits were beginning to close when a never-to-be-identified voice broke in: "Fuck Flabby."

We swung south out of the Yangtze River and picked up a pilot to lead us up the Whang-Po (now called the Huangpu) River to our dock in Shanghai. I could see the *St. Paul* from where we moored. I had business there but first I wanted to see the town. Shanghai was still under the pall of years of Japanese oppression. I have seen recent pictures of this flourishing modern city. It bears no resemblance to the poverty-stricken town I saw in 1945. For one thing, there was a currency problem. Shanghai, and possibly other Chinese cities, were in the grip of runaway inflation. A currency exchange took my U.S. dollars and handed me a bundle of strange looking paper money that made my pockets bulge. A few of my destroyer shipmates joined me in hiring a guide, an affable young native who spoke English as well as I did. He took us to a restaurant decorated like the more expensive Oriental restaurants I have seen in Chicago and San Francisco. I had expected the cuisine to be the same as what I'd seen in those restaurants but I was surprised. The waiter brought the mandatory pot of tea along with what I took to be an appetizer. Both were very good. The guide did his best to describe Shanghai to us foreigners while we waited for the entrée. Instead, the waiter brought us another appetizer—also very good. We talked, drank tea, and the waiter brought more appetizers. Our guide called for the check and I was surprised to see that we had been dining for three hours—on a seven course dinner. Good food. Good service. I tipped the waiter 10,000 yuan.

Shanghai nightlife didn't measure up to the level of the restaurant. Waterfront night spots with their nondescript music

The Shanghai Bund, 1946 (People's Republic of China, public domain)

were no different than those we hung out in on the other side of the world. The best entertainment was an extemporaneous show on the Bund, a crowded, broad thoroughfare near the Whang-Po. There were no taxis in the town but there were plenty of rickshaws for hire. One night, waiting for a ride back to the dock, I heard an outbreak of cheering. A pair of rickshaws were speeding down the Bund. A race, but like no race I had ever seen. Two bewildered and frightened coolies were perched on the seats of their rickshaws while a pair of sweating, panting sailors labored in the shafts. The crowd shouted encouragement as they swept by. I didn't see the finish but I'm sure thousands of yuan changed hands. The high octane levity of the sailors couldn't mask the ugliness of wartime Shanghai. The drab buildings and the poorly lighted streets were an appropriate background for the human debris, survivors of years of violence and poverty. Our personnel truck stopped briefly on its return to the docks. A starving girl in a filthy dress climbed into the truck to offer her services to the lot of us. A chief sitting near the tailgate gave her a thousand yuan and sent her on her way.

Having had a taste of Shanghai nightlife, I was ready to move on. I boarded the *St. Paul* and showed my orders to a clerk in the flag office. I tried to make a case for a quick trip to Great Lakes. I was tired of my life as a military drifter. What I wanted was to have my separation papers in one hand and my final paycheck in the other. I made my pitch to the transportation officer. I told him I had done my time, and then some, when you consider my four months in Shangri-La. "All you have to do," I told him, "is put me on the fastest vehicle heading for Chicago." It wasn't that easy. Several million servicemen and women were asking for the same thing. Washington had worked out a point system for discharging the veterans that gave the highest priority to age and marital status. Accumulated battle stars and years of service came next. I apparently made some impression. He promised to get me on the first vessel moving east. I knew air travel was out of the question but I had reason to hope for some kind of ship that cruised at 18 knots.

I made my obligatory visit to the *St. Paul* a few days later and the transport officer told me that he had an ARL leaving for Pearl Harbor that afternoon. I didn't even ask him what an ARL was. I assumed it was one of those cruiser-like ships designed for special weapons. I packed my gear and hitched a jeep ride to a group of Navy ships a mile and a half up the shore. "Where's ARL 18?" I asked a passing sailor. "You're standing right in front of it," he told me. Couldn't be. The ship I was standing in front of was an LST. But the sailor was right. When I took the trouble to look at the bow I saw the big, white lettering ARL 18. The ship was an LST alright, built in Seneca, Illinois, but sometime in its career it had been converted to a floating machine shop, complete with lathes, power drills and milling machines covering her tank deck. A seaman showed me to my cabin, a 5' x 8' cubicle with an upper and lower bunk. I threw my gear on the upper bunk and went out on deck to watch the crew handle the lines as we cast off. The pilot had to swing the ship 180 degrees to get her headed down the Whang-Po. By evening we had entered the Yangtze and were standing down the famous river and out into the East China Sea.

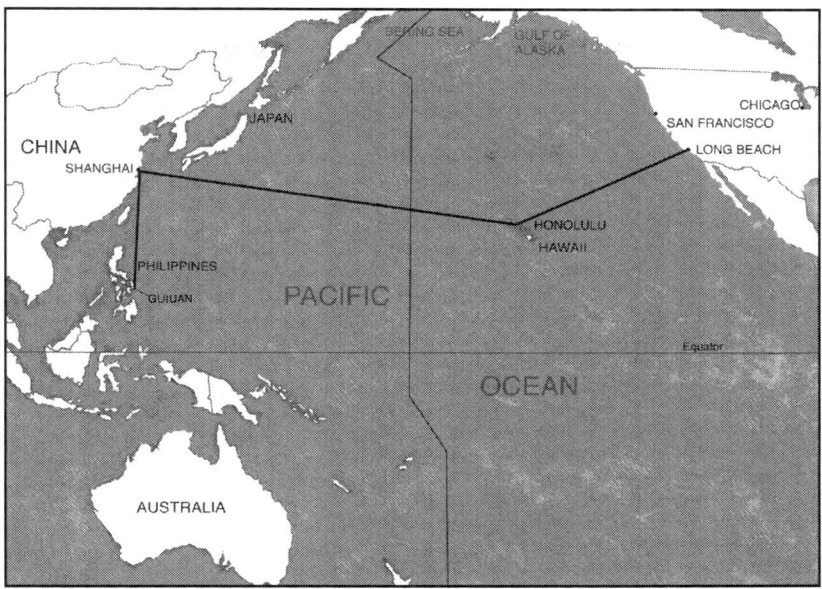

Long Journey Home, February–April 1946

Unlike the "old man" on LST 400, the skipper of ARL 18 (USS *Pandemus*) really was an old man by our youthful standards. He was a 42-year-old mustang, Navy talk for a chief petty officer commissioned for wartime duty, usually to serve as a commanding officer. He was short of experienced deck officers and asked if I'd be willing to stand watch. Actually he could have ordered me to do it. I was glad to help out. It beat playing cribbage for the next couple of weeks. The skipper was "old Navy" and that's the way he ran his ship. He was no Captain Bligh, but he *did* go by the book. One morning at breakfast he complained about the prunes: too hot, too dry, whatever. They looked OK to me but the old man got worked up enough to call for the chief commissary steward and chewed him out in front of the gathered officers and mess boys. I was struck by the similarity between the skipper and the chief. Both were lean, sandy-haired men in their forties; both had spent their adult life in the Navy. But circumstances placed one in absolute command of the other. The same circumstances, at war's end, would place them back on even footing. I wonder if they ever met eye to eye as peacetime equals.

Pearl Harbor Entrance, 1940 (National Archives: 80-G-411119)

The officers of the USS *Pandemus* were a congenial group—all but one. This was an ensign who kept to himself and apparently had no specific duties. I inquired to learn that he was under arrest and was being taken back to Pearl Harbor for court martial. The charge was homosexuality. I greeted him from time to time but kept my distance. This was the 1940s and I shared the homophobia of the times.

The highlight of that trans-Pacific crossing was a talk I had with the supply officer. Make that "supply officer." This guy wasn't the usual deck officer who handled the ship's supplies as a collateral duty. This was a member of the Navy Supply Corps. I stress this because he was authorized to handle payrolls. In casual conversation, I told him about my wanderings from Great Lakes to Shanghai without ever finding my ship. "You must have piled up some real 'per diem,'" he said. My ears pricked up. "What's 'per diem?'" He told me that officers traveling on orders were granted a daily expense allowance. I can't recall the exact number, say $7 per day. When I told him of the time that elapsed between the day I picked up my orders and the day I reported on board the *St. Paul*, he was amazed. Probably a new record for an officer in transit. I had the feeling that he was sorry that he had brought the subject up. But he told me he'd make the application when we reached Pearl Harbor.

Pearl Harbor was crowded with ships and Honolulu was crowded with servicemen. The government was doing its damnedest to return its soldiers and sailors to civilian life, but there were still a lot of us on hand in March 1946. Wandering about Honolulu I ran across a few familiar faces, including that of old shipmate Al Krezdorn, now a Lt (jg). On the island of Oahu I fell easily into my open-mouthed tourist routine. I followed the coastline from Kahuku Point to Diamond Head. The remnants of the December 7, 1941 onslaught were still to be seen but I didn't care to examine them too closely. My sightseeing ended when the captain of the *Pandemus* told me the ship was leaving for Panama in a few days. Normally a trip to Panama would suit me fine but not at the cost of a few more weeks on the open sea. The skipper agreed to release me if I found a quicker passage home and I soon fell back into the "check-in every morning" routine. But this time the odds were on my side. On the second day the duty officer put me on a destroyer heading east and the following week I was walking along a pier in Long Beach, baggage in hand, looking for a taxi to take me to downtown L.A. The date was April 2, 1946, and Great Lakes was only 1,500 miles away.

Railroad passenger service was at its peak in the 1940s and I had the choice of riding to Chicago on the Santa Fe Chief, the Union Pacific's City of Los Angeles or the Burlington Zephyr. Airlines were becoming more available by this time but I was partial to rail travel, a carryover from the days when I used to ride about northern Illinois with my grandfathers, neither one of whom drove a car. I don't remember which one of the new diesel powered, streamliners I chose but I was soon rolling through the mountains of California and then the deserts of

City of Los Angeles *(Union Pacific Museum, with permission)*

Arizona. Passengers got on and off at Flagstaff and Albuquerque. One of them tried to sell me life insurance; another tried to save my soul. It was great to be home. I crossed prairies and streams and then, the greatest river of them all, the Mississippi. I was back in Illinois. The train carried me through hometown Geneva doing 50 miles per hour. No matter. I had business in the great metropolis. A short run up to Great Lakes where my separation from the Navy was brisk and brief. I say "separation" because I wasn't discharged from the Navy for another 20 years. My final day ended on a high note. My supply officer buddy on the *Pandemus* had come through. In addition to my accumulated back pay, I was given a $1,500 per diem allowance. I headed for Geneva with about $2,000 in my pocket, a helluva lot of money in 1946. In terms of present-day dollars, it comes to about $21,000. On that happy note my involvement with history came to an end. In the year 2010, sixty-four years later, I can't say that World War II has ever completely left my mind.

What I've written here are the recollections of one man, among hundreds of millions, involved in the greatest devastation the modern world has known. Nature has delivered great blows to the people of this planet but this one mankind inflicted on itself. The death count is usually set above fifty million. Some say more. But the misery of human existence went beyond the death count alone. In relating bits and pieces of the whole, I am surprised to see how easily I could move from the gut-wrenching experience of killing our airborne soldiers at Sicily to a frivolous caper with wine bottles in Oran, from hauling wounded off the Normandy beaches to a night at the theater in London, from the wretchedness and squalor of Shanghai's destitute to a lavish meal at the city's finest restaurant. Only the very young can do that.

Jaeger Family Home, Geneva, Illinois (courtesy of the author)

Fox River, Looking South from Geneva Bridge (courtesy of Betsy Lawson)

Geneva Public Library (courtesy of John J. Laukaitis, Ph.D.)

State Street Looking East, Geneva, Illinois (courtesy of John J. Laukaitis, Ph.D.)

"1942"

"1944"

"1946"

Top: courtesy of CB&I. Middle: National Archives: SC 489601.
Bottom: courtesy of the author.

Made in the USA
Lexington, KY
21 December 2018